# About Island Press

Since 1984, the nonprofit Island Press has been stimulating, shaping, and communicating the ideas that are essential for solving environmental problems worldwide. With more than 800 titles in print and some 40 new releases each year, we are the nation's leading publisher on environmental issues. We identify innovative thinkers and emerging trends in the environmental field. We work with world-renowned experts and authors to develop cross-disciplinary solutions to environmental challenges.

Island Press designs and implements coordinated book publication campaigns in order to communicate our critical messages in print, in person, and online using the latest technologies, programs, and the media. Our goal: to reach targeted audiences—scientists, policymakers, environmental advocates, the media, and concerned citizens—who can and will take action to protect the plants and animals that enrich our world, the ecosystems we need to survive, the water we drink, and the air we breathe.

Island Press gratefully acknowledges the support of its work by the Agua Fund, Inc., Annenberg Foundation, The Christensen Fund, The Nathan Cummings Foundation, The Geraldine R. Dodge Foundation, Doris Duke Charitable Foundation, The Educational Foundation of America, Betsy and Jesse Fink Foundation, The William and Flora Hewlett Foundation, The Kendeda Fund, The Andrew W. Mellon Foundation, The Curtis and Edith Munson Foundation, Oak Foundation, The Overbrook Foundation, the David and Lucile Packard Foundation, The Summit Fund of Washington, Trust for Architectural Easements, Wallace Global Fund, The Winslow Foundation, and other generous donors.

The opinions expressed in this book are those of the author(s) and do not necessarily reflect the views of our donors.

# Reshaping Metropolitan America

METROPOLITAN PLANNING + DESIGN

*Series editors: Arthur C. Nelson and Reid Ewing*

A collaboration between Island Press and the University of Utah's
Department of City & Metropolitan Planning, this series provides a
set of tools for students and professionals working to make our cities
and metropolitan areas more sustainable, livable, prosperous, resilient,
and equitable. As the world's population grows to nine billion by
midcentury, the population of the United States will rise to one-half
billion. Along the way, the physical landscape will be transformed.
Indeed, two-thirds of the built environment in the United States at
midcentury will be constructed between now and then, presenting a
monumental opportunity to reshape the places where we live. The
Metropolitan Planning + Design series presents an integrated approach
to addressing this challenge, involving the fields of planning,
architecture, landscape architecture, urban design, public policy,
environmental studies, geography, and civil and environmental
engineering. The series draws from the expertise of some of the
world's leading scholars in the field of Metropolitan Planning + Design.

Please see Islandpress.org/Utah/ for more information.

OTHER BOOKS IN THE SERIES:

*The TDR Handbook,* Arthur C. Nelson, Rick Pruetz,
    and Doug Woodruff (2011)
*Stewardship of the Built Environment,* Robert Young (2012)
*Governance and Equity,* Marc Brenman and Thomas W. Sanchez (2012)
*Good Urbanism: Six Steps to Creating Prosperous Places,* Nan Ellin (2012)
*Measuring Urban Design,* Reid Ewing and Otto Clemente (2013)

ARTHUR C. NELSON

# RESHAPING

# METROPOLITAN AMERICA

Development Trends
and Opportunities to 2030

 **ISLAND**PRESS

Washington | Covelo | London

ISLAND PRESS is a trademark of the Center for Resource Economics.


Library of Congress Cataloging-in-Publication Data

Nelson, Arthur C.
  Reshaping metropolitan America : development trends and opportunities to 2030 / Arthur C. Nelson.
    p. cm. — (Metropolitan planning + design)
  Includes bibliographical references and index.
  ISBN 978-1-61091-019-4 (cloth : alk. paper) — ISBN 1-61091-019-2 (cloth : alk. paper) — ISBN 978-1-61091-033-0 (pbk. : alk. paper) — ISBN 1-61091-033-8 (pbk. : alk. paper)   1. City planning—United States.   2. Urban renewal—United States.
3. Land use, Urban—United States.   I. Title.
  HT167.N396   2012
  307.760973—dc23

                          2012025625

Printed on recycled, acid-free paper

Manufactured in the United States of America
10  9  8  7  6  5  4  3  2  1


Cover Image: The Noma Development Strategy was designed for The Cultural Development Corporation of the District of Columbia

The data in this book adapted from Woods & Poole Economics, Inc. (copyright 2011) is subject to its End User License Agreement including warranties, limitations and disclaimers (the End User License Agreement is provided at www.WoodsandPoole.com). The data are not authorized for use in legal or financial transactions. No warranties and/or representations of any kind are made regarding information or data provided. In no event, shall the author, publisher, Woods & Poole Economics, Inc., or their/its agents or any other person or entity be liable in any way to the users of this data. No party warrants or guarantees the data for any particular purpose.

KEYWORDS: Accessory dwelling units, American Dream, Baby Boomers, compact development, development trends, Eisenhowers, fertility rates, Gen X, Gen Y, iGeneration, Great Recession, home ownership, land use regulations, Millennials, mixed-use, multigenerational households, NIMBY, population trends, Reshape America Index, revitalized suburbs, smart growth, sustainable communities, telecommuting, transit-oriented development, YIMBY

*To Monika and Emily,*

*who have journeyed with me across America witnessing*

*how the built landscape is in a constant state of change.*

# CONTENTS

Foreword | xi

Acknowledgments | xiii

INTRODUCTION | 1

1 MAJOR MARKET TRENDS AND DEMOGRAPHIC CHANGES | 9

2 WHAT AMERICANS WANT | 33

3 HOUSEHOLDS AND HOUSING | 47

4 SPACE NEEDS FOR JOBS | 67

5 THE RESHAPE AMERICA INDEX | 81

6 THE BENEFITS OF RESHAPING METROPOLITAN AMERICA | 89

7 AGENDA TO RESHAPE METROPOLITAN AMERICA | 109

Notes | 123

References and Selected Bibliography | 133

Index | 143

# FOREWORD

*Congressman Earl Blumenauer (OR-03)*

America's metropolitan landscape is undergoing a profound transformation. The Baby Boomers who have driven the nation's economy since the end of World War II will have turned sixty-five by 2030, and they will demand different kinds of housing than that in which they grew up and raised their own families. Many millions will want smaller homes on smaller lots, attached options, and walkable neighborhoods. The generations that follow them—Gen X, Gen Y, and the Millennials—will actually have a larger influence on future housing demand than Boomers, and many millions of them have even less affinity for the standard suburban home. These emerging trends in housing will profoundly reshape America's metropolitan areas. Those regions and communities that grasp the nature and magnitude of emerging changes in the housing market will be best equipped to re-invent themselves, becoming more liveable places.

At the same time, most of America's nonresidential building stock will become ripe for redevelopment because the buildings themselves will be worth less than the land under them. Because two-thirds of all buildings in the United States are one or two floors, almost all of them will be replaced or in some way converted from their original use. Importantly, most of the land on which these buildings sit is devoted to parking. Indeed, most new residential and nonresidential development can go on these parking lots with plenty of asphalt left over; existing developed land can accommodate most of the future growth.

Emerging markets will transform America's metropolitan areas; the question is how? Even if all new homes built between now and 2030 were within walking distance of transit stations, the market demand for walkable transit accessibility would still not be met. The one major challenge facing policy makers, developers, and planners is to invent new ways of extending transportation options to meet emerging market needs. Doing so will reshape metropolitan areas by significantly reducing demand for land, energy, and new infrastructure.

This book documents Americans' changing preferences for housing, neighborhoods, and transit options and what those changes mean for planning and development. It provides market demand estimates for new and replaced housing units and nonresidential uses for every metropolitan and micropolitan area in the nation. It demonstrates the extent to which all new development could be accommodated on the footprint of existing parking lots. Arthur C. Nelson shows how future growth could thereby meet emerging market demands and thus expand economic development, reduce pressure to develop greenfields, and reduce local fiscal burdens.

There is no better time than the present to reshape America's metropolitan areas so they are ready for 2030 when the last Baby Boomer reaches retirement age. Planners, developers, elected officials, and citizens need this critical information if we are to meet the demand for livable communities in the coming decades.

# Acknowledgments

It is impossible to properly acknowledge all the people who have helped me shape the themes and analysis presented in this book. Foremost, I am indebted to Heather Boyer of Island Press for her extraordinary help in shaping *Reshaping Metropolitan America*. I am also indebted to Sharis Simonian for her deft editing of sometimes dense material. I cannot thank them enough for their careful eye on details and clear mind on what we are trying to accomplish with this book.

Reshaping Metropolitan America started as a journey during my stint in 2000–2001 as a special advisor to Susan Wachter, presently at the Wharton School of the University of Pennsylvania but then US Department of Housing and Urban Development (HUD) assistant secretary for policy development and research. Her support helped me frame the initial questions about where demographic and economic forces were taking the nation's economy into the next century.

A special thanks is due to Bruce Katz, who provided key support for my first full version of key concepts, published by the Brookings Institution's Metropolitan Policy Program as *Toward a New Metropolis: The Opportunity to Reshape America* (Nelson 2004). I am indebted as well to Amy Liu and Rob Puentes, also at Brookings. Joe Molinaro at the National Association of Realtors was also complicit in those early days and is a champion of evidence-based smart growth policies.

I am especially grateful to Christopher B. Leinberger for his unique perspectives on how our markets are continually changing. The homes we build this year will last nearly two centuries (sometimes longer), but will they meet housing demands of those generations? Chris (and this Chris) seeks to answer that question.

Numerous other friends have helped me shape the arguments in this book. Greg Ingram and Armando Carbonell at the Lincoln Institute of Land Policy gave me numerous platforms to present earlier versions of my work. The feedback at these events was invaluable. Peter Calthorpe of Calthorpe Associates; Amanda Eaken of the Natural Resources Defense Fund; Uwe Brandes, Matthew Johnston, Trisha Riggs, and Elizabeth Razzi of the Urban Land Institute; and Kate White, now with the San Francisco Foundation, lent ways to frame the data analysis for lay and professional audiences. Lee Sobel, John Thomas and Kevin Ramsey at the Environmental Protection Agency also provided key insights. I owe special thanks to Robert E. Lang, now at the University of Nevada at Las Vegas but my former colleague and co-director of the Metropolitan Institute at Virginia Tech for especially clear insights on trends and their implications. A special thanks as well to Dowell Myers of the University of Southern California for sharing important demographic insights with me over the past quarter century.

Support for much of the work appearing in this book has come from many sources over the years. In addition to those mentioned elsewhere, I am indebted to Geoff Anderson and Ilana Pruess at Smart Growth America and Don Chen at the Ford Foundation.

Haya el Nassar at *USA Today* brought earlier versions of my work to the world's attention. This led to numerous invitations by Christopher H. Cole, president and CEO of Cole Capital, to share emerging analysis in this field. Along the way, Bernard Winograd, of Prudential Real Estate, helped me to further flesh out analysis and implications, as have Clark Ivory of Ivory Homes, Roger Boyer of The Boyer Company and Chris Lee of CEL Associates.

A special debt is owed to Gregg Logan and Shyam Kanan of RCLCO for lending me access to and insights from their in-house analysis of trends. Their work inspired many of the ideas developed in this book.

Academic and professional help from HUD over the years is also acknowledged. In addition to Dr. Wachter, special thanks is owed to

Shelley Poticha and Mariia Zimmermann of HUD's Office of Sustainable Housing and Communities.

My students at Georgia Tech, Virginia Tech, and now the University of Utah, often suffering through interminable expositions on the nuances of development data, helped me refine the message that the America of our (mostly *their*) future will be nothing like the past.

My colleagues suffered as well, so I am especially pleased to acknowledge that Reid Ewing, Nan Ellin, Keith Bartholomew, Stephen Goldsmith, Phil Emmi, and Brenda Scheer—my colleagues at the University of Utah—helped and humored me along the way. I am especially indebted to Michael Larice, also at Utah for providing extraordinarily constructive insights.

I am grateful for the permission granted to me by Woods & Poole Economics, Inc., to use their data for key calculations reported in this book.

But for the office management dedication of Myriam Lechuga when I was at Virginia Tech and Jeannette Benson at the University of Utah, where I am presently, I cannot fathom how I could have finished this book and fulfilled my managerial responsibilities. I am also grateful to Derrick Bingman and Don Burris for their endless (and often off-hours) IT support, as well as to Jenny Lind and Sue Wolfe for their managerial support.

A further debt of gratitude goes to my staff at the University of Utah, especially Martin Buchert and Dejan Eskic for assembling databases, J. P. Goates for crafting the figures, and Sarah Hinners for key insights. Susie Petheram, Gail Meakins and Matt Miller provided additional data collection, assembly and insights.

Over the years (actually decades), I have received invaluable insights and counsel from Jim Nicholas, emeritus professor of planning and law at the University of Florida, Julian Juergensmeyer, Ben F. Johnson Jr., Chair in Law at Georgia State University and professor emeritus of law and planning at the University of Florida, and Dwight Merriam, partner with Robinson and Cole and adjunct professor of law at the University of Connecticut and the Vermont Law School. Gentlemen, thank you.

When it comes to comprehending the sweeping changes occurring right under our noses, very few of our elected leaders at any level of government "get" the implications. Thankfully, a few do, especially Earl Blumenauer, member of Congress from Oregon's third Congressional district. I am grateful for his foreword.

This book would not have been possible without the encouragement of hundreds of professionals, elected officials, and engaged citizens who in their own way gave me insights on how to shape my message. Thank you, all.

Arthur C. Nelson
*Salt Lake City, Utah*

# INTRODUCTION

More than $20 trillion will be spent on reshaping America's metropolitan areas between 2010 and 2030. Because of the Great Recession, nearly all of it will be spent after about 2015. The amount of new and replaced or repurposed nonresidential space nationally will nearly equal all the space existing in 2010—nearly eighty billion square feet. New and replaced residential units will be about a quarter of all units existing in 2010—more than thirty million units.

Will America after the Great Recession continue the sprawling development patterns that characterized metropolitan growth after World War II? *No.* A key reason is monumental shifts in housing preferences fueled by Boomers (born 1946–1964) and Gen Y (born 1980–1999), who together account for more than two-thirds of the nation's housing demand. They want something different.

The Baby Boom of the mid-twentieth century combined with unprecedented home financing inventions, massive infrastructure investments, and antiurban policies fueled American-style suburban sprawl for a half century. For tens of millions of households, the "American Dream" was seen as owning a detached home on a large lot far away from, well, everything. It was during this time that the United States became a "suburban nation" (Duany et al. 2000). A number of factors were at work. One was the availability of mortgage instruments allowing for small down payments with loans paid over decades, thus facilitating home ownership (Schwartz 2007). However, to qualify for federally insured mortgages, buyers usually had to purchase homes in

1

developments meeting federal regulations, such those affecting subdivision design (Jackson 1987). Second, federal, state, and local financial regulations, incentives, and planning decisions clearly favored single-family, detached homes, often on large lots, over attached homes or even detached homes on small lots. In part because of these factors, the United States saw the greatest change in home ownership rate seen in the nation's history, rising from a low of 43 percent in 1940 during the depths of the Great Depression to 66 percent in 2000 and in 2010.[1]

These new car-oriented developments were too low density to sustain public transit, even if that was a desired option at the time. For instance, the density of cities with more than thirty thousand people fell from about 6,500 persons per square mile in 1950 to about 3,700 per square mile in 2000.[2] Over the period from 1950 into the 1990s, America's land use and development patterns were aimed at accommodating the preferences of the Baby Boomers at that time—large lot, sprawling, auto-oriented suburban landscapes. The conventional zoning template, in which land uses are separated from one another, owes itself to facilitating expansion of single-purpose residential developments throughout suburban America principally to provide for a mostly child-oriented society (Nelson 2006). By 2010, more than half of America's homes sat on more than one-sixth of an acre; fewer than 30 percent of the nation's homes were in attached combinations.

When confronted with choices between large homes on large lots with long commutes and small homes on small lots with short commutes, a poll commissioned by the National Association of Realtors (NAR) found that nearly 60 percent Americans now want the latter option (Belden Russonello & Stewart 2011), with most of the demand coming from Baby Boom and Gen Y households. Another survey indicates that the ideal home size is less than two thousand square feet for one-third of individuals polled compared to only 9 percent of Americans who say their ideal size is more than 3,200 square feet (Trulia-Harris Interactive Survey, 2010).

The NAR surveys show that about 39 percent of American households polled what attached housing options (apartments, condominiums, cooperatives, townhouses, multiplexes), about 37 percent want small-lot options (not necessarily small homes), and just 24 percent want large-lot options.[3] In contrast, the American Housing Survey shows that only about 30 percent of the nation's occupied housing units are attached, about 20 percent (smaller than one-sixth acre) are small lots, and about half of all homes sit on larger lots, which I call "conventional" lots[4]—about thirty million more than there appear to be demand.

These surveys show further that about half of Americans want to live in walkable communities with mixed housing and other mixed uses; they want to be able to walk to grocery stores, pharmacies, restaurants, and the like. We might call these "smart growth" communities (Belden Russonello & Stewart 2011; see also Handy et al. 2008). More than half, 56 percent, of Americans surveyed selected the smart growth option, while 43 percent preferred the sprawl option. Moreover, 59 percent of Americans would choose a small home on a small lot with a commute of less than twenty minutes over a large house on a large lot with a commute of more than forty minutes.

We also know from surveys that about half of all Americans want transit options (Handy et al. 2008). In addition, about a quarter of Americans want the option of walking or biking to work, as well as for errands (Handy et al. 2008). But will they "walk the walk" when given the opportunity? It turns out that when people live within a mile of work, nearly 40 percent walked or biked to work in 2009—up from 25 percent as recently as 1995. When people live or work within a mile of errands, more than 40 percent walked or biked for this purpose—up from 26 percent in 1995.[5] If we could provide all Americans who want the opportunity to walk or bike to work and for errands, and by implication provide them with the housing opportunities they prefer, greenhouse gas emissions may be reduced substantially.

The benefits of meeting emerging market demands are considerable. Environmental benefits include lower carbon emissions and reduced dependence on fossil fuels; protection of open space through lower rates of greenfield development and increased human health from walking/biking/transit options, along with lower emissions. Economic benefits include stimulating private investment in areas that will generate more economic return through economic synergies, which will in turn increase jobs and wages; increased property values and in turn more stabilized values over time as areas become more resilient to economic downturns; fiscal resilience as local economies become less reliant in unsustainable single-use, low-density urban forms; and "green" jobs that require less energy and produce less pollution per job than the current average. There are also social benefits that include greater opportunity for social engagement; the potential to provide affordable housing by minimizing transportation costs; and improving the accessibility of low income households to economic opportunity and services.

It will not be easy to steer America's built-environment "ship" in a new direction. After all, in a typical year, about 1.5 million new housing units are built in the United States. If no new homes were built on large lots between 2010 and 2030, there would still be an excess supply of large lots relative to demand. Given the imbalance between supply and demand, the value of homes on large lots in America's suburban fringe and exurbs has plummeted.

In contrast, markets in the center of metropolitan areas will be where values increase the most. Consider metropolitan Atlanta, Georgia, considered one of the most sprawling metropolitan areas in the nation. In the years since the Great Depression ended officially, housing values within or in communities adjacent to Atlanta's I-285 perimeter freeway rose while they continued to fall in suburban areas and even more in exurban areas.[6] As I point out in chapter 7, America's central cities are increasing their share of metropolitan residential construction, much of it at higher densities than suburbs and accessible to transit.

In this book I explain why I believe that between 2010 and 2030 most of America's nonresidential space will be replaced either through demolition and reconstruction, or repurposing through renovation and rehabilitation. Combined with changing preferences for housing types and accessibility options, there is an opportunity to reshape America's commercial corridors and centers from mostly low-intensity, single-purpose urban forms to higher-intensity mixed-use ones that will help to house the next sixty-five million Americans between 2010 and 2030, and respond to changing market preferences. Will developers and planners take advantage of this opportunity? Only if the accommodation of market trends is facilitated through a range of federal, state, and local policy initiatives. Indeed, virtually all the demand for new development between 2010 and 2030 can be met by redeveloping existing commercial corridors and centers, including the parking lots that dominate those spaces.

Understanding how we can get from where we are now to where market trends are headed is the purpose of *Reshaping Metropolitan America: Development Trends and Opportunities to 2030*.

The particular time period is chosen for the simple reason that between 2011 and 2029 America's Baby Boom generation will have turned sixty-five. Between 2010 and 2030, the share of the population over sixty-five will increase from 13 percent to 20 percent, and will remain about 20 percent for several decades thereafter.

*Reshaping Metropolitan America* includes seven chapters, and additional information is available at www.ReshapeMetroAmerica.org, including tables that expand upon the data offered in the book. Chapter 1 identifies key market trends that will reshape the housing market especially between 2010 and 2030, such as rising energy prices, stagnating incomes, shifting wealth, more rigorous home purchase underwriting standards, and demographic changes. It also shows sweeping demographic trends that will reshape housing demand, from aging Baby Boomers, to rising dependency of old and young people on a shrinking labor force (aged sixteen to sixty-five), to greatly expanding racial and ethnic diversity. It also identifies trends facing the nonresidential built environment.

Chapter 2 reviews preference surveys showing emerging market-based demand for more compact locations with shorter commutes and more community amenities, such as the ability to walk to local places. I will show a very large mismatch between what it is people say they want in surveys for different housing types and what the actual supply is.

Chapter 3 addresses households and housing. It shows, among other things, that only 14 percent of the growth in households between 2010 and 2030 will have children living in them and thus 86 percent will not (because the children have already been raised, have yet to be raised, or in some cases will never be raised), and more than half of the growth in households to 2030 will consist of single persons—mostly as Baby Boomers loose their partners. It also shows that the time when America's housing market was dominated by households at their peak income and space needs has run its course.

Chapter 4 is about space-occupying jobs, the space they need, and redevelopment of rapidly depreciating space. It begins with an assessment of the kinds of jobs that occupy space, estimates the new space needed to serve those jobs and, most important, estimates that, nationally, more than half the volume of nonresidential space existing in 2010 may be replaced, renovated, or in other ways repurposed for more intensive and/or different functions between 2010 and 2030.

Because the largest share of existing space sits on vast seas of parking lots that, if redeveloped, would reshape America, chapter 5 presents the Reshape America Index. It shows that, for most of America, all new growth could be accommodated along existing low-intensity commercial corridors and nodes. These corridors may not now have transit services, but with modest increases in jobs and housing, consistent with emerging market trends, they can move from being "transit-ready" to "transit-served."

Chapter 6 casts a vision of what America might be like if all new development occurred in existing developed areas, especially along commercial corridors and nodes. The evidence suggests that, compared to having that development sprawl farther out, benefits would include $4 trillion or more in ecosystem service values retained, lower unemployment and higher wages, more resilient local fiscal structures, and more social benefits.

In chapter 7, I pose an agenda for reshaping America that includes democratizing who can be allowed to live in homes, abandoning tax policies that have socially engineered society resulting in the inefficiencies that are robbing the nation of economic and personal health, reforming how we pay for local public facilities and services, and rightsizing our permitting practices to avoid calamities that we saw in the 1980s relating to overbuilding of commercial space—leading in large part to the collapse of the savings and loan industry (Nelson 1995)—and in the 2000s when we overbuilt our residential stock—leading in large part to the Great Recession.

*Reshaping Metropolitan America* is not about thwarting the option to live in homes on large lots away from centers; indeed those options are more plentiful than ever before and at affordable prices if we ignore transportation costs. It is rather about expanding choices for the one-third to one-half of Americans who do not want single-family detached homes on large lots isolated from services, jobs, and people. Those Americans want walkable communities and the ability to walk or bike to work or for errands. Yet, even if all new housing and nonresidential development built between 2010 and 2030 were in locations that one-third to one-half of Americans preferred, the market demand would still not be met. But America and its metropolitan areas would still be better off.

# 1

# Major Market Trends and Demographic Changes

In recent years, home ownership has become a feature of the American Dream. This was not always the case. Historically, the American Dream was characterized as people being rewarded fairly for their effort and each new generation being better off than the prior one (Adams 1931). The dream has evolved to include home ownership for reasons that are not entirely clear (Rohe and Watson 2007). Fulfillment of that part of the dream has been largely achieved. Since the end of World War II, home ownership in the United States rose from 55 percent in 1950[1] to 69 percent in 2004.[2] By 2030, however, it will may be less attainable or even desirable. Reasons for this include rising energy costs, falling incomes, lagging employment, shifting wealth to upper classes, and tighter mortgage underwriting requirements. Added to these reasons are market trends including key population and sweeping generational changes, the rise of a new housing market, and important nonresidential trends. These trends and changes will lead to a new America in 2030.

## RISING ENERGY COSTS

One key reason for the rise in home ownership has been the vast supply of inexpensive land available for home building outside cities.

Another reason is that the cost of driving to work and other destinations was inexpensive because of cheap gasoline prices. This has changed.

Since the early 2000s, energy prices have been rising steadily (Energy Information Administration 2012), which makes supporting a home more expensive. It also makes locations far away from work, shopping, and other destinations more expensive because of vehicle fuel costs. For instance, from the early 2000s to the early 2010s, the national average price of a gallon of gasoline rose about 10 percent per year, compounded.[3] At this rate, gasoline prices will exceed eight dollars per gallon by 2020 and more than twenty dollars per gallon by 2030.[4] Higher gasoline prices might be offset by more fuel-efficient vehicles, but they are more expensive than conventional vehicles.

Steadily increasing gasoline prices dampen the attractiveness of suburban fringe and exurban areas for home buying. For instance, a study for the Federal Reserve Board by Molloy and Shan (2011) showed that, after a four-year lag, a 10 percent increase in gasoline prices decreases the demand for homes by 10 percent because of longer average commuting times relative to locations closer to jobs, a highly elastic outcome. On the other hand, homes closer in are usually more expensive to purchase. Without new approaches to mortgage underwriting, the overall effect of rising gasoline prices will be fewer households able to both buy homes and pay for gasoline (see chapter 7).

## FALLING INCOMES

Incomes are falling in real terms. For instance, median household incomes for all age groups in each income category ended the 2000s lower than in 2000 (Harvard Joint Center for Housing 2011, 15). Along with falling incomes, America's household wealth in 2010 had fallen to levels not seen since the 1990s. Indeed, the Federal Reserve Board (2012) reported that median family net worth wealth fell from $126,400 in 2007 to $77,300 in 2010. In constant 2010 dollars, family net worth was at about the 1992 level.

Moreover, the poverty rate increased from 11.3 percent in 2000 (Dalaker 2001) to 15.1 percent in 2010 (DeNavas-Walt et al. 2011).

The rate of increase appears to be fastest in the suburbs. Over the period 2000–2008, suburbs accounted for nearly half the increase in the population in poverty (Kneebone and Garr 2010). In contrast, primary cities accounted for just over 10 percent of the increase. Suburbs may be especially hard-hit because of rising gasoline prices (see above) and lagging employment (see below). These trends may further alter housing demand over the next several decades (McKeever 2011).

## LAGGING EMPLOYMENT

It is not just that the unemployment rate spiked during the Great Recession of 2008–2009 and remained high well into the 2010s, but that the structure of the nation's labor force makes it prone to higher unemployment. A key feature of employment and income is preparedness based on education. Unfortunately, black and Hispanic students lag behind white[5] students in reading and mathematics; indeed since the 1990s the gap has not been narrowed.[6] As minorities increase their share of the nation's labor force, the nation could be challenged with developing enough talent to compete in the global market. The implication also is that the ability of workers in the future to afford homes may be compromised. Indeed, during the 2010s, whites will make up just 12 percent of the growth in the nation's labor force, followed in increasing order by Asians (16 percent), blacks (18 percent), and Hispanics (54 percent). As the nation's future labor force becomes less prepared through shortcomings in the education system, wages may be lower and unemployment rates higher by historical standards.

## SHIFTING WEALTH

The nation's wealth has been shifting steadily to a smaller percentage of more households. In the 1980s, about 80 percent of the nation's wealth was held by the wealthiest fifth of America's households. By 2009, nearly 99 percent of America's wealth was held by the same quintile.[7] The Great Recession and its aftermath can be blamed for reducing much of the wealth of the middle and lower classes. Historically, a large share of wealth in American households has been the equity in their homes. However, much of this was removed by the Great Recession, as homeowners lost a third of their equity. Moreover, on average, homeowner equity has fallen steadily since 1945, from about 85 percent to about 40 percent.[8] The reason is the advent of highly leveraged home purchase opportunities that became widely available during the past generation. The Great Recession changed this, however, making buying homes more difficult.

## WANING INSTITUTIONAL SUPPORT FOR HOME OWNERSHIP

The Great Recession of 2008–2009 was caused in large part by the bursting of the "housing bubble" of the mid-2000s. Some banks and other financial institutions were closed forever, millions of homes were foreclosed or "sold short" to avoid foreclosure, and home equity saw its biggest decline since the Great Depression of the 1930s. How did this happen? One factor (others will be discussed later) was "subprime" mortgages, in which people with insufficient credit could still buy a home, often with no money down and sometimes with money back, such as buying with no money down a $200,000 home that appraised for $250,000. Most of these subprime mortgages came with very low initial rates on adjustable rate mortgages, often around 3 percent, that would rise every six to twelve months until parity was achieved with a target index, often the London Interbank Offered Rate (LIBOR), plus two points (a 6.5 percent mortgage pegged to a 4.5 percent LIBOR). The trouble is that mortgage payments often doubled, or more, rising beyond the ability of households to afford them. But it was not just credit-challenged households; the low rates of adjustable rate mortgages attracted millions of existing home owners to refinance, only to fall into a similar predicament.[9]

In the wake of this financial disaster have come numerous changes. In response to the recession, lending institutions initially increased their underwriting requirements, thereby reducing the number of people who could qualify to a buy a home. Since then, the financial market for mortgage underwriting has undergone a sea change. Home buyers who would have formerly qualify for conventional mortgages are facing higher credit score, work history, and down-payment requirements. The move to make the 20 percent down payment once-again standard for conventional mortgages issued by lending institutions regulated by the federal government draws this concern from the National Association of Home Builders:

> Requiring a high down payment would disproportionately harm first-time home buyers, who have limited wealth and on average account for 40 percent of home-buying activity. It would take an average family 12 years to scrape together a *20 percent down payment*. Borrowers who can't afford to put 20 percent down on a home and who are unable to obtain FHA financing will be expected to pay *a premium of two percentage points* for a loan in the private market *to offset the increased risk to lenders,* according to NAHB economists. This would *disqualify about 5 million potential home buyers,*[10] resulting in 250,000 fewer home sales and 50,000 fewer new homes being built per year.[11] (italics added)

For context, about two-thirds of all American households with mortgages in 2009 put less than 20 percent down for their home.[12] Clearly, higher down payment requirements will reduce the number of households that can afford to buy a home. The home ownership rate may fall.

Between the mid-2000s and mid-2010s, American real estate lost more than six trillion dollars in value, or almost 30 percent. Up to one in five American homeowners found themselves owing more on a mortgage than what their home was worth.[13] Analysis of the value of homes reported by the National Association of Home Builders shows that between 2000 and 2011, the average value of all homes in the United States fell in real terms.[14] Although home ownership remains an important element of the nation's economy, there is also an emerging sense among prospective homebuyers to be cautious. For instance, the National Foundation for Credit Counseling summarized results of a 2009 survey it commissioned as follows (Cunningham 2009: 1):

"The lack of confidence in consumers' ability to buy a home, improve their current housing situation, or trust homeownership to provide a significant portion of their wealth sends a strong message about the impact of the housing crisis. It appears that whether a person was directly affected or not, Americans' attitudes toward homeownership have shifted."

The survey also found that:

- Almost one-third of those surveyed do not think they will ever be able to afford to buy a home.
- Forty-two percent of those who once purchased a home, but no longer own it, do not think they will ever be able to afford to buy another one.
- Of those who still own a home, 31 percent do not think they will ever be able to buy another home (upgrade existing home, buy a vacation home, etc.).
- Seventy-four percent of those who have never purchased a home feel that they could benefit from first-time homebuyer education from a professional.

The combination of tighter mortgage lending and disillusionment in home ownership as a sound investment seems likely to push ownership rates down. National home ownership rates peaked in the mid-2000s and have declined since, and are expected to continue to fall, with the only question being how far. For instance, the Urban Land Institute (McIlwain 2009) projected that the home ownership rate in 2020 would range between about 62 percent and 64 percent.

The rate of home ownership is largely a function of household income and the ability to make a down payment. Home ownership was pushed to its limits in the mid-2000s, reaching an all-time high of about 69 percent in 2004. This was achieved through subprime loans, allowing people to buy homes without qualifying for them in the traditional sense; "Alternative-A" loans, allowing people meeting marginal qualification standards to buy a home; and extensive use of "jumbo" loans, allowing people to borrow more than the Federal Housing Administration limits. These modes of financing are either gone or highly restricted. Conventional home financing, reminiscent of the period from the 1950s into the mid-1990s, is now about the only way to buy a home, and may likely be the case in the coming decades. The effect will be to push down home ownership rates and increase demand for rental housing. Changes to the ability to buy homes will especially hit hard on minority households. Here is why:

Between 1965 and 1995, the median home ownership rate was about 64 percent. This was a blended average based on a society composed mostly of white households. Between 2000 and 2010, however, the home ownership rate did not change much. The overall rate stayed at 67 percent, and for whites it stayed at 74 percent. For blacks it went down from 47 percent to 45 percent, while for Hispanics it rose slightly from 46 percent to 47 percent.[15] It may be unlikely that those rates will change much.

If we assume the home ownership rate for all major racial and ethnic groups in 2010 remains the same until 2030, the nation's ownership level will fall to about 64 percent because of increasing shares of minority groups. If home ownership falls to about 64 percent, then the demand for rental housing may increase at a faster pace than population growth. Indeed, rental housing will account for about 55 percent of the growth and owner housing for about 45 percent. However, holding 2010 home ownership rates constant to 2030 may be optimistic, given the underwriting trends reviewed earlier. If the home ownership rate for each racial and ethnic group is just 5 percent lower in 2030 than in 2010—moving from 74 percent to 70 percent for whites, for instance—the nation's overall home ownership rate will fall to about 61 percent, the same it was in the 1960s. Rental housing will account for about 75 percent of the new housing demand with owner housing accounting for just 25 percent.

The bottom line is that between 2010 and 2030, (1) fewer people may be able to buy homes, (2) those who own homes may not be able to refinance to help pay the down payment on a new home for their children, and (3) fewer home buyers may further drive down demand and thus prices, which may further erode equity.

As an element of the American Dream, home ownership may be reverting to the lesser role it played before World War II (Kamp 2009).

## KEY POPULATION TRENDS

The makeup of America's population in 2030 is going to be vastly different compared to 2010. To show this, I use the Woods & Poole Economics (2011) projections to 2030 (table 1.1)[16] for the nation, the census regions and divisions showing this. There are few surprises. States and metropolitan areas located in the South and West census regions will see the greatest share of growth, accounting for about 80 percent of the nation's growth.[17] What may also be surprising to some are key aging, minority and dependency trends.

*Table 1.1* Population of the nation, census regions and divisions, 2010–2030 (figures in thousands).

| Geographic area | Population 2010 | Population 2030 | Change | Percent change (%) | Share of change (%) |
|---|---|---|---|---|---|
| United States | 309,350 | 373,924 | 64,575 | 21 | |
| *Census regions* | | | | | |
| Northeast | 55,361 | 60,490 | 5,129 | 9 | 8 |
| Midwest | 66,976 | 74,374 | 7,398 | 11 | 11 |
| South | 114,866 | 147,794 | 32,928 | 29 | 51 |
| West | 72,147 | 91,267 | 19,120 | 27 | 30 |
| *Census divisions* | | | | | |
| New England | 14,457 | 16,234 | 1,776 | 12 | 3 |
| Mid Atlantic | 40,904 | 44,256 | 3,353 | 8 | 5 |
| East North Central | 46,439 | 50,747 | 4,309 | 9 | 7 |
| West North Central | 20,537 | 23,626 | 3,089 | 15 | 5 |
| South Atlantic | 59,923 | 77,435 | 17,512 | 29 | 27 |
| East South Central | 18,458 | 22,153 | 3,695 | 20 | 6 |
| West South Central | 36,485 | 48,205 | 11,721 | 32 | 18 |
| Mountain | 22,137 | 29,723 | 7,587 | 34 | 12 |
| Pacific | 50,010 | 61,544 | 11,534 | 23 | 18 |

*Source*: Adapted from Woods & Poole Economics, Inc. (2011).
*Note*: Percentages may not sum due to rounding. For details, see www.ReshapeMetroAmerica .org.

## Aging Trends

Nationally, the number of children (under eighteen years of age) will increase by 17 percent, but it will be seniors, principally Baby Boomers, whose population will grow the fastest—nearly 80 percent, as shown in table 1.2. Seniors as a share of total population will increase from about 13 percent in 2010 to 19 percent in 2030. They will comprise nearly half the share of population change over this period—32 million of the nation's increase of 65 million in population.

## Minority Trends

Even more dramatic will be the change in the nation's racial and ethnic composition. Table 1.3 shows that the minority population will grow by more than 50 percent and will account for 86 percent of America's overall population growth. Moreover, in the New England, Mid Atlantic, and Pacific census divisions, thirteen states, and dozens of metropolitan areas, minorities will account for all or nearly all the population change (see the detailed demographic tables at www .ReshapeMetroAmerica.org).

## Dependency Trends

America will also become more "dependent." A concept called the "dependency ratio" compares the share of population in the work force (aged sixteen to sixty-five) to children (those under eighteen years of age), seniors (those sixty-five and older), and both groups. The higher the ratio, the more workers are needed to support dependents. Table 1.4 shows the dependency ratio trends over the period 2010 to 2030.

In most areas of the nation, the dependency ratio for children will increase, albeit slightly. This is because more children will be born during these twenty years than during prior decades, which itself is attributable to Gen Y and early Millennial persons moving into child-bearing and child-rearing age. The significant change in dependency ratio will be with respect to seniors, because of Boomers turning sixty-five between 2011 and 2029, increasing 62 percent nationally and about that across all geographic units.

*Table 1.2* Senior population for the nation, census regions and divisions 2010–2030 (figures in thousands).

| Geographic area | Population 65+ (2010) | Population 65+ (2030) | Change in population 65+ (2010–2030) | Percent change in population 65+ (2010–2030, %) | Share of change within geographic area (%) |
|---|---|---|---|---|---|
| United States | 40,331 | 72,337 | 32,006 | 79 | 50 |
| *Census regions* | | | | | |
| Northeast | 7,810 | 12,681 | 4,871 | 62 | 95 |
| Midwest | 9,027 | 14,850 | 5,823 | 65 | 79 |
| South | 14,926 | 27,841 | 12,915 | 87 | 39 |
| West | 8,568 | 16,966 | 8,397 | 98 | 44 |
| *Census divisions* | | | | | |
| New England | 2,043 | 3,668 | 1,624 | 80 | 91 |
| Mid Atlantic | 5,767 | 9,013 | 3,246 | 56 | 97 |
| East North Central | 6,213 | 10,193 | 3,980 | 64 | 92 |
| West North Central | 2,814 | 4,658 | 1,843 | 65 | 60 |
| South Atlantic | 8,354 | 15,627 | 7,273 | 87 | 42 |
| East South Central | 2,473 | 4,211 | 1,738 | 70 | 47 |
| West South Central | 4,099 | 8,003 | 3,904 | 95 | 33 |
| Mountain | 2,696 | 5,385 | 2,688 | 100 | 35 |
| Pacific | 5,872 | 11,581 | 5,709 | 97 | 49 |

*Source*: Adapted from Woods & Poole Economics (2011).
*Note*: Percentages may not sum due to rounding. Percentages of more than 100 percent mean decline in younger age population with seniors accounting for both the decline and all remaining growth.

The increasing dependency ratios may challenge American society as fewer workers will be available to support more dependents. But this assumes Boomers will retire in their sixties which, according to Glaeser (2011b), may not happen. Indeed, in earlier generations seniors were on the whole less healthy than current seniors, and employers encouraged retirement earlier to make room for plentiful younger workers who would command a lower wage. Given labor-force short-

*Table 1.3* Minority population of the nation, census regions and divisions, 2010–2030 (figures in thousands).

| Geographic area | Minority population 2010 | Minority population 2030 | Change (2010–2030) | Percent change (2010–2030, %) | Share of change within geographic area (%) |
|---|---|---|---|---|---|
| United States | 107,438 | 163,087 | 55,649 | 52 | 86 |
| *Census regions* | | | | | |
| Northeast | 16,513 | 24,013 | 7,500 | 45 | 146 |
| Midwest | 13,867 | 20,059 | 6,193 | 45 | 84 |
| South | 44,531 | 69,604 | 25,072 | 56 | 76 |
| West | 32,527 | 49,411 | 16,884 | 52 | 88 |
| *Census divisions* | | | | | |
| New England | 2,766 | 4,680 | 1,914 | 69 | 108 |
| Mid Atlantic | 13,747 | 19,333 | 5,586 | 41 | 167 |
| East North Central | 10,665 | 14,899 | 4,234 | 40 | 98 |
| West North Central | 3,202 | 5,161 | 1,959 | 61 | 63 |
| South Atlantic | 22,719 | 36,208 | 13,488 | 59 | 77 |
| East South Central | 4,761 | 6,859 | 2,098 | 44 | 57 |
| West South Central | 17,050 | 26,537 | 9,486 | 56 | 81 |
| Mountain | 7,296 | 12,263 | 4,967 | 68 | 65 |
| Pacific | 25,231 | 37,148 | 11,917 | 47 | 103 |

*Source*: Adapted from Woods & Poole Economics, Inc. (2011).
*Note*: Percentages may not sum due to rounding. Percentages greater than 100 mean decline in white population with minorities making up for the decline and accounting for all remaining growth.

ages and the decades of experience seniors have, it may well be that seniors have the choice of working well into their seventies. They might even be willing to work for less income (perhaps for fewer hours) because in their seventieth year they automatically receive social security, often at the highest income possible, plus many will have individual retirement accounts that federal laws require they draw down over their anticipated remaining lives. The combination of social security,

Table 1.4 Senior, child, and total dependency ratios for the nation, census regions and divisions.

| Geographic area | Senior dependency ratio 2010 | Senior dependency ratio 2030 | Percent change in senior dependency ratio (2010–2030, %) | Child dependency ratio 2010 | Child dependency ratio 2030 | Percent change in child dependency ratio (2010–2030, %) | Total dependency ratio 2010 | Total dependency ratio 2030 | Percent change in total dependency ratio (2010–2030, %) |
|---|---|---|---|---|---|---|---|---|---|
| United States | 19.4 | 31.5 | 62 | 35.8 | 37.9 | 6 | 55.2 | 69.4 | 26 |
| **Census Regions** | | | | | | | | | |
| Northeast | 20.8 | 34.2 | 64 | 32.9 | 35.1 | 7 | 53.8 | 69.3 | 29 |
| Midwest | 20.2 | 32.9 | 63 | 36.2 | 38.8 | 7 | 56.4 | 71.7 | 27 |
| South | 19.4 | 30.6 | 57 | 36.3 | 38.3 | 5 | 55.7 | 68.8 | 24 |
| West | 17.6 | 30.2 | 71 | 36.9 | 38.6 | 4 | 54.5 | 68.7 | 26 |
| **Census Divisions** | | | | | | | | | |
| New England | 20.7 | 37.3 | 80 | 32.0 | 33.8 | 6 | 52.8 | 71.1 | 35 |
| Mid Atlantic | 20.9 | 33.1 | 58 | 33.3 | 35.6 | 7 | 54.1 | 68.7 | 27 |
| East North Central | 20.0 | 33.0 | 65 | 35.9 | 37.9 | 6 | 55.9 | 70.9 | 27 |
| West North Central | 20.7 | 32.8 | 58 | 36.7 | 40.7 | 11 | 57.4 | 73.5 | 28 |
| South Atlantic | 20.8 | 32.9 | 58 | 34.3 | 36.4 | 6 | 55.1 | 69.3 | 26 |
| East South Central | 20.0 | 30.9 | 54 | 35.8 | 38.5 | 7 | 55.8 | 69.4 | 24 |
| West South Central | 16.9 | 26.7 | 58 | 39.7 | 41.1 | 3 | 56.6 | 67.8 | 20 |
| Mountain | 18.4 | 29.6 | 61 | 39.0 | 40.5 | 4 | 57.4 | 70.1 | 22 |
| Pacific | 17.2 | 30.4 | 76 | 36.0 | 37.6 | 4 | 53.3 | 68.0 | 28 |

Source: Adapted from Woods & Poole Economics, Inc. (2011).
Note: Percentages may not sum due to rounding.

retirement income, and the ability to continue working may be especially attractive to many millions of seniors.

## SWEEPING GENERATIONAL CHANGES

There will also be sweeping generational changes. Boomers will turn sixty-five by 2030. Whites will become less dominant; indeed virtually all population growth to 2030 will be attributable to racial and ethnic minorities. Household composition will also change: where about half of American households included children during the Baby Boom years of 1946 to 1964, by 2030 only about a quarter of households will have children. Each of these generational trends will have its own unique impact on America's built environment, especially housing demand.

*A Nation of Generations*

Since the end of the Baby Boom era, America has become increasingly a nation of households without children living in them. In 2000, roughly one-third of American households had children and in 2030 slightly more than a quarter will. Because people are living longer than ever before, the American population will be composed of a few very large and roughly equally sized age groups, each with its own unique housing needs. The populations for each generation living in 2010 and projected to live in 2030 are reported in table 1.5. The reader will see that I have named one future generation for reasons I describe later. I will not presume my names for them will be the ones that come into popular use, but I needed to name them now for purposes of this book. Those generations and their housing needs are reviewed next.

**Eisenhowers**–People born before 1946. There will be about eight million of them living in 2030, down from about forty million in 2010. They will comprise about seven million households. People in this generation will be more than eighty-five years old and live in downsized units, assisted living, nursing homes, with kith or kin, or in other forms of group housing.

**Baby Boomers**–People born between 1946 and 1964. In 2010 there were about eighty-two million Boomers and in 2030 they will number about sixty-four million living in about thirty-eight million households. The American Association of Retired Persons notes that about 90 percent of seniors would prefer to "age in place," and about 80 percent believe they can do so in their current residence (Keenan 2010). If they are unable to age in place, they will be actively downsizing, with many millions moving into assisted living, nursing homes, living with kith or kin, or in other forms of group housing. Many millions who may want to move into homes more suitable to their life stage may not be able to. For them, aging in place will be a necessity for longer than they might have anticipated (see Cisneros et al. 2012). Many millions will also find that limited transportation options mean that they are "stuck in place" (Transportation for America 2011). In my view, Boomers will force the transformation of the urban landscape (Nelson 2009). As a group they may demand more smart growth communities than other age groups, as I discuss in the next chapter.

**Gen X**–People born between 1965 and 1980. There will be about sixty-two million of them in 2030, roughly the same as were living in 2010. Their households will number about thirty-four million. Being fifty to sixty-five, this age group will be at the peak of their earning power and likely choosing to live in the most expensive housing of all age groups, whether McMansions in the suburbs or condominiums in high-rise towers in downtowns and all the major forms of owner-occupied housing in between. But this age group will also consist mostly of empty nesters or those soon to become empty nesters, and they will begin to seek different types of housing than they have now, and in different locations.

**Gen Y**–People born between 1981 and 1995. In 2030 they will number about seventy-one million and include about thirty-eight million households. Being aged thirty-five to forty-nine, they will be the group most demanding of larger homes with good (usually suburban) public school systems.

**Millennials**–People born between 1996 and 2010. In 2030, they will also number about seventy-one million living in about twenty-six million households, mostly small families and singles. They are just starting out in adult life and their housing needs will mostly be apartments and small starter homes. Many millions may remain with their parents until their late twenties or early thirties, or longer.

Two other generations will emerge between 2010 and 2030. Based on work by New Strategist but not exactly using their time frame, the iGeneration will include about seventy-four million people born between 2011 and 2025.[18] Although Boomers represented about a quarter of the nation's population when they were born, the iGeneration will comprise a large share in their own right—about one-fifth. They will account for a very small number of households in 2030, however, as nearly all of them will still be with their parents while a smaller number will be away from home in school, military or other service, or in other group quarters. The generation after them, born between 2026 and some later year, will be named by others when the time is appropriate. They will number about twenty-three million in 2030. The middle four groups—Boomers, Gen X, Gen Y, and Millennials, will dominate the housing market to 2030. Two groups, Gen X and Gen Y, will seek housing principally for raising families; they will be in their peak housing demand stage of life. Totaling more than sixty million households, they will account for slightly less than half of the 143 million households projected for 2030. With twenty-seven

Table 1.5 Population by Generation, 2010–2030 (figures in millions).

| Generation | 2010 | 2030 |
| --- | --- | --- |
| Eisenhower (pre-1946) | 40 | 8 |
| Baby Boom (1946–1964) | 82 | 64 |
| Gen X (1965–1980) | 61 | 62 |
| Gen Y (1981–1995) | 65 | 71 |
| Millennial (1996–2010) | 61 | 71 |
| iGeneration (2011–2025) | 0 | 74 |
| Unnamed Generation (2026–?) | 0 | 23 |
| Total | 309 | 374 |

Source: Population figures adapted from Woods & Poole Economics (2011).
Note: Percentages may not sum due to rounding.

million households, Millennials will comprise about a fifth of the housing demand in 2030. Boomers, who were raised in households that accounted for more than half of all households in the 1950s, will comprise about a quarter of all households in 2030. Roughly three-quarters of the housing demand in 2030 will be for households without children because they have already raised children (mostly Boomers and Gen Xers), have not yet raised children (mostly New Millennials and many Gen Yers), or may never raise children. I will elaborate on these trends and their implications in chapter 3.

In large part because of the aging Boomers, the number of households without children will dominate household growth. Households headed by a single person will be the fastest growing market segment. One reason is that people are living longer, and as Boomers age they will dominate growth of the single-person segment. Another major change will be in the racial composition of households. Minority household growth will be six times that of white households. These changes, combined with others, will have profound effects on America's future housing markets. Just how profound is open to speculation, including mine, which are shared in this book.

Through the history of the United States (and much of the world), the distribution of the population was like a pyramid with younger people making up the largest share of the population, and thus the pyramid base, with successively older groups making up smaller shares until the very top included the oldest people and the smallest share of the population. This is changing. Between 1970 and 2030, the nation's population pyramid will have shifted decidedly from the traditional pyramidal form to one that is more cylindrical. In 1970, 46 percent—nearly half—of the population was under age twenty-five, but in 2030 this age group will account for 32 percent—about a third—of the population. At the other end of the age spectrum, only 10 percent of the population was over sixty-five years of age in 1970, but in 2030, 19 percent will be. This age group will increase 2.5 times in size between 2010 and 2030, and will account for nearly a third of the nation's shift in population by age. Indeed, those turning sixty-five between 2010 and 2030 will account for half of the change in population distribution over those two decades.

Just as the age composition of the American population is changing dramatically so is its racial and ethnic composition. In 2010 the white population was nearly two-thirds of the nation's population, but by 2030 it is expected to account for only 14 percent of the nation's growth. In other words, 86 percent of America's growth over the period 2010–2030 will come from minority races and ethnicities. Most of the growth will come from Hispanics of all races, including white, black, Asian, and other.

Let us also consider average household size. For more than a century, the average household size in the United States has been falling. Starting at 4.60 persons per household in 1900, average household size fell steadily to 2.59 persons per household in 2000.[19] There are many reasons for this, including: (1) women are delaying or forgoing marriage and are thus increasingly older when they have children, and they have fewer children; (2) more women are raising children outside of marriage; (3) more people are moving from rural to urban environments, which generally weakens and even ends the need for extended families; (4) the education of women leads to more women in the workforce and to delayed marriage, with associated lower birth rate; and (5) since the 1960s women have had improved birth control (Downs 2003; Goldin 2004). But the trend of falling household size has stopped.

Declining household size means more homes are needed for the same population. For instance, one million people in 1900 would have occupied about 217,000 homes, but in 2000 they would occupy about 386,000 homes. Between 1950 and 2000, the combination of population growth with declining household size made for a robust home-building industry. During this period, the population grew by 87 percent while the number of occupied housing units increased by 144 percent. Put differently, for every two new residents in the United States one new home had to be built.

But that trend has changed. Average household size was 2.58 in 2010,[20] nearly the same as in 2000. The trend toward ever-declining household size seems to have stopped and might even be reversed in future years. In effect, during the 2000s, fewer homes needed to be built than actually were.

Although the Great Recession, with its lingering effects into the mid-2010s, could be blamed for this, in fact other dynamics are at work. Principal reasons for increasing number of persons per household include rising fertility rates and households doubling up into larger units.

Consider fertility rates. Demographers consider that a fertility rate of 2.1 sustains a population; a rate higher than this means the population is growing while a lower one means it is falling. Indeed, the nation's fertility hit an all-time low of 1.7 in 1976, but it has risen steadily since. By the late 2000s, the fertility rate had climbed back to 2.1.

Thus, after decades of falling average household size fueled in large part by decades of falling fertility rates, trends have changed. One reason for the increasing fertility rate is the changing ethnic composition of America, especially influenced by Hispanics, given the higher fertility rate among Hispanic women relative to women of other selected ethnicities (Martin et al. 2009).

In 2000, Hispanics accounted for about 12.5 percent of the US population but their share rose to about 16 percent in 2010. In part for this reason, Hispanics accounted for half of the nation's growth during the decade.

Another reason for the increasing fertility rate is that more women are having children at later ages than earlier generations (Hamilton et al. 2009). In 1976, nearly all babies were born to women under thirty. Controlling for age, the fertility rate of women under thirty years of age was less than 1.5, while for women over thirty it was about 0.3. By the end of the 2000s, the fertility rate of women under thirty had not changed since 1976, but for women over thirty it had increased to nearly 0.7. In other words, the entire increase of the fertility rate between 1976 and the end of the 2000s may be attributable to women having children after thirty.

Another important trend is the rise of multigenerational households (Taylor et al. 2010). These are households that include two generations with parents (or in-laws) and adult children aged twenty-five and older; three generations: parents (or in-laws), adult children (and spouse), and grandchildren; "skipped" generation with grandparents and grandchildren, without parents (including stepchildren); or more than three generations (Pew Research Center 2010, 2). Since 1980, the number and share of Americans living in multigenerational households rose to forty-nine million and 16 percent in 2008, respectively. The trend since 1980 is seen among adults of all ages, especially the elderly and the young.

As Boomers enter retirement age in unprecedented numbers, combined with growth in the population almost entirely among racial and ethnic minorities, the number and share of multigenerational households would seem destined to increase—by how much has not been explored. My extrapolation of trends from 1980 to 2010 indicates that about 20 percent of Americans will be in multigenerational households by 2030, but it may be closer to what was seen in 1900, or about 24 percent.

All these trends lead to the most sweeping change of all. For its entire existence, the United States was a nation mostly of households with children. As I will show in chapter 3, by 2030, slightly more than a quarter of American households will have children. Even more remarkable is this: between 2010 and 2030, households with children will account for about 13 percent of the total change in households; households without children will represent the rest. Single-person households will account for half of the change in households, about four times more than those with children. A key reason for this is Boomers who will turn sixty-five in unprecedented numbers during this period, many millions of whom will loose their partners.

## THE NEW HOUSING MARKET

All these factors point to lower home-ownership rates and higher average household size by 2030 than was projected in 2000 for 2010 and 2030. Overall, fewer new housing units will be needed and more of them will need to be for renters. Also, location will matter even more in the future than in the past because homes farther away from centers are unlikely to appreciate. There may be little or no demand for homes in exurban or suburban fringe areas of slow-growing or stagnating metropolitan areas. Current occupants of those homes may need to walk away from them. In table 1.6, I develop a matrix showing home value trends among metropolitan areas with different growth rates (the columns) and different value outcomes over time. There will be exceptions to the outcomes in any given cell, but the overall pattern may be consistent with changing market factors. The bottom line for home owners and home buyers of the future is that values will be preserved and possibly enhanced only by purchasing homes in closer-in urban and suburban locations. This does not rule out buying homes farther away or in the exurbs, but they should be purchased for the lifestyle choice with little expectation of value appreciation.

There is something else going on. That is an emerging housing market for homes with multiple household options. The Urban Land Institute (2011) says it best:

> Although monster McMansions go the way of Hummers, ample-sized suburban homes may come back into vogue sooner than we think. Houses with multiple bedrooms and bathrooms are well suited to accommodate an expected increase in multigenerational living arrangements, as more families pool resources. Grandparents facing shrinking retirement savings or forced into early retirement can take care of grandkids, eliminating child care costs, while both parents work to help make ends meet. Adult kids, some married and with children, move back in with parents and stay longer as well-paying jobs become harder to land. Immigrant families—Hispanic, East and South Asian, African, Russian—characteristically open their homes to relatives and friends of relatives as they gain economic footholds. When you add multiple incomes together, houses at lower price points may become reasonable and monthly mortgage payments possible. Various forms of "doubling up"—cohabitation, roommate, and sibling living arrangements—will incubate, too. (p. 37)

There is another trend: In their analysis of the American Housing Survey, Eggers and Moumen (2011) found that nearly 20 percent of America's housing stock switched from owner to renter occupancy between 1985 and 2009. I suspect that share will increase to 2030.

*Table 1.6* Home value changes to 2030 based on growth rates and location.

| Location | Faster than US growth rate | About US growth rate | Slower than US growth rate | Stagnating or declining |
|---|---|---|---|---|
| Downtown/ near downtown | Highest value increase | Increasing value | Holding value | Losing value |
| Elsewhere in central city | High increasing value | Increasing value | Holding value | Weak market |
| Suburbs built to about 1980 | Holding value | Holding value | Weak market | Little or no market |
| Suburbs built 1980s to about 2000 | Holding value | Losing value | Little or no market | No market |
| Post-2000 suburbs | Losing value | Weak market | Little or no market | No market |
| Exurbs | Little or no market | No market | No market | No market |

| Cell Descriptor | Description |
|---|---|
| Highest value increase | Appreciation faster than the national population growth rate. |
| High increasing value | Appreciation somewhat higher than the national population growth rate. |
| Increasing value | Appreciation at about the national population growth rate. |
| Holding value | Small losses; niche markets might gain some value. |
| Losing value | Losing value; unless they discount modestly to sell, sellers will "chase the market down." |
| Weak market | Only niche markets work; sellers need to discount heavily. Consider renting out the home. |
| Little or no market | Very few niche markets work; sell if willing to take considerable losses. Consider renting out the home. |
| No market | Live in the home as long as practicable; rent out home if there is a rental market; consider walking away eventually. |

*Note:* There will be exceptions to these general patterns.

## NONRESIDENTIAL DEVELOPMENT TRENDS

In 2010, the United States had about one hundred billion square feet of nonresidential space serving about 190 million workers (full- and part-time). More than 80 percent of this space was in structures of one or two floors with a floor-area ratio—the ratio of building space to land area—of about 0.20 or less. By 2010, about a third of this space was ripe for development. Because of the Great Recession much of this has not happened. Between 2010 and 2030 fifty billion square feet will become ripe for renewal. In other words, by 2030, with up to 60 percent of the nonresidential stock existing in 2010 will become ripe for conversion. There may be an unprecedented opportunity to convert aging nonresidential development sitting mostly on large, flat chunks of land along transit-ready collectors, arterials, and expressways into higher and better uses that meet emerging housing and nonresidential development needs. I will discuss this more in chapter 4.

## A NEW AMERICA EMERGES, 2010–2030

It goes without saying that the United States will be a different place in 2030 than in 2010. Amplifying this is a report by the Urban Land Institute (2011) identified key trends facing the real estate industry through the rest of the 2010s and into the 2020s. Paraphrased and with some additional insights, those key trends follow.

- Average household income began falling even before the Great Recession and individual retirement plans have been compromised. These factors, along with loss of home equity, stress households and this is not going to change much during the 2010s. Developers will need to invent new products and financing tools to meet the needs of financially strained households (p. 32).
- Rising energy prices and increasing congestion will increase the demand for locations and real estate developments that offer live-work options, less driving, or enhanced opportunities to work at home (p. 15).

- Multifamily development demand will focus around public transit stations and near suburban centers. Over time, single-use commercial strips will be turned into mixed-use corridors. Local officials and planners have an opportunity to partner with developers to create multiuse projects in and around existing shopping malls and office parks (p. 34).
- If they can sell their homes to Gen X and Gen Y, affluent Boomers will downsize out of larger suburban homes and seek locations with convenient urban lifestyles; many will move into condominiums and townhouses (p. 38).
- Boomers as a whole will seek walkable places, especially those with accessibility to grocery stores and medical offices. Public transit will become crucial for getting around, especially given increasing energy prices and constrained budgets (p. 74).
- Gen Y will reshape urban markets. Though most of them will want the same kinds of homes they grew up in as they raise their children, up to a third will want something much different from their Boomer parents. Priced out of many close-in neighborhoods, however, often by Boomers, Gen Y will settle for redeveloping commercial corridors and nodes along transit routes convenient to jobs (p. 39).
- On the other hand, as Boomers and Gen Y seek more urban living options, gentrifying close-in neighborhoods, low income households will be pushed into the weakening outer suburban rings where the housing and commercial stock is degenerating. Urban blight will be turned on its head, becoming suburban blight (p. 41).
- Urban redevelopment is shifting to the suburbs where vast supplies of asphalt make for attractive development opportunities. Developers and planners, often in partnership, will need to retool dead and dying shopping malls and retail strips, repurpose suburban fringe and exurban subdivisions hammered by foreclosures, and reconsider already-approved greenfield developments (p. 65).
- The new economy also pummels local fiscal bases, a situation further exacerbated by cuts in federal and state support. No longer

can we afford to subsidize high-cost development at the suburban fringe. As streets and highways, utilities, and public buildings run their useful lives, how and even whether to reinvest in them will dominate future public works discussions. At the same time, as suburbs become more densely settled, people will need more parks and open spaces (pp. 15–16, 65).

- These trends create new forces that planners, developers, and investors can marshal to recreate urban and suburban places and transit corridors to increase housing and transportation choices. Walkable neighborhoods around commercial centers will make public transit feasible, reduce vehicle miles traveled, and lower the household transportation cost burdens (pp. 64–65).

Do Americans embrace these changes and challenges? In the next chapter, I will show that, according to preference surveys, they do.

# 2

# What Americans Want

A merica may be in for a rude awakening over the next few decades. The Baby Boomers came into their own during the 1980s
through the 2000s. Their affluence and need for space was matched by
developers who provided low-cost products across America's landscape. Boomers accounted for about three-quarters of the demand for
all new housing during this period, and America became a truly suburban nation.

That was then and this is now. The Boomers are now becoming
empty nesters and will begin downsizing by the millions over the next
few decades. Though millions will choose to age in place so long as they
can, many other millions want something different. Millions of Boomers will want to exchange their large homes on large lots in distant,
automobile-dependent, and isolated suburbs for smaller homes on
smaller lots, or attached options, closer to destinations and with multiple ways of getting around (see Nelson 2010).

As Boomers change their housing choices, Gen Y will emerge as
the next dominant influence on the housing market. Gen Y, those
born between 1981 and 1995, will number about seventy-one million
people in 2030 and will enter the peak of their housing needs between
the 2010s and 2030s. By 2030, Gen Y will comprise about thirty-three
million households whose heads of household will range in age between thirty and fifty. We are learning that many millions of them
do not necessarily want to live in the kinds of homes, neighborhoods,
or communities where their parents raised them. A third or more

want the very kinds of options empty-nesting and downsizing Boomers want.

Along with aging Boomers, the emerging housing preferences of Gen Yers will reshape America's communities, but how?

A 2011 National Association of Realtors survey (Belden Russonello & Stewart 2011, cited hereafter as "NAR 2011") of smart growth preferences asked more than two thousand respondents to trade off attributes between two prototype communities. This survey was designed and executed to avoid eliciting respondent bias relating to pejorative word phrases. Respondents were given a choice between two community types (A and B). Neither community was labeled as "smart growth" or "sprawl." In its design, Community A is the implicit "sprawl" choice, while Community B is the implicit "smart growth" choice. The community types were these:

> Imagine for a moment that you are moving to another community. These questions are about the kind of community you would like to live in. Please select the community where you would prefer to live.
>
> **Community A**–Houses are built far apart on larger lots and you have to drive to get to schools, stores and restaurants, park/playgrounds, and recreation areas, or
>
> **Community B**–Houses are built close together on smaller lots and it is easy to walk to schools, stores and restaurants, parks/playgrounds, and recreation areas

More than half, 56 percent, of Americans surveyed selected the smart growth community (option B) while 43 percent preferred the sprawl option. Those choosing the smart growth option did so mostly because of the ability to walk to shops and restaurants (60 percent) while those choosing the sprawl option did so because it provided single-family detached homes (70 percent). RCLCO's demographic analysis of the NAR survey found that among thirty-five– to fifty-four–year-old respondents, representing those in their peak child-rearing years, 54 percent preferred the smart growth option (RCLCO 2011).

Walking is clearly an important neighborhood feature, with 66 percent saying it is very or somewhat important to be within an easy walk of places in deciding where to live. For specific destinations, this varies from 75 percent to be able to walk to a grocery store, 65 percent to walk to a pharmacy, 61 percent to walk to a hospital, and 60 percent to walk to restaurants.

The NAR survey (2011) showed that although a majority of Americans desire space and privacy, 59 percent would choose a smaller house and lot if it meant a commute time of twenty minutes or less.

## BOOMERS AND NEW URBANISM

Between 2011 and 2029, America's Baby Boom population will turn sixty-five. Just as their presence reshaped America's built environment in the 1950s through the 1990s, so will they reshape it over the next generation. This section pays special attention to the effect Boomers will have on the built environment to midcentury. Indeed, I call the period from 1946—the beginning of the Baby Boom—to the middle twenty-first century the Baby Boom Century because those born during the boom will have reshaped America at every stage of their life. Nearly eighty million babies were born between 1946 and 1964, equivalent to about half the nation's population in 1950. America's suburbanization between 1960 and 1980 is attributable largely to their housing and educational needs that arguably could not have been met in the cities at the time (Bruegmann 2005). To meet their higher education needs, America's colleges and universities expanded as never before, with enrollment increasing from two million to more than fifteen million between 1950 and 2000.[1] To cater to the housing and educational needs of their children (Gen Y, born between 1981 and 1995), America's suburbs spread even farther out. As Boomers turn sixty-five, between 2011 and 2029, and downsize, they will leave behind millions of suburban homes that no longer meet their needs. Because of Boomers' changing housing needs, there will be more sellers of homes in the 2020s than buyers in most states (Myers and Ryu 2008). The trend started during the early 2010s because of the bursting housing bubble, but it would have happened by the mid- to late 2010s anyway. I call the pending flood this Great Senior Sell-Off.

From the 2020s to midcentury, Boomers will shift America's housing market toward senior-oriented options, in very large numbers. Those options include smaller homes on smaller lots or attached products; more walkable neighborhoods with grocery, drug, medical, and other destinations within walking distance of homes; and more mobility options, such as walking, biking, short-distance driving, and transit (see Nelson 2010). The share of the population consisting of seniors will rise from about 13 percent in 2010 to about 19 percent in 2030, and then remain at about that level to at least midcentury (ARA 2011, 2).[2] Although comprising a fifth of the population, they will account for a third of the nation's new housing demand to midcentury because the average household size of seniors is about 1.76 inhabitants compared to 2.60 for the rest of the population.[3]

However, between 2010 and 2030, Boomers will actually account for about 60 percent of the change in demand for housing. As Pitkin and Myers (2008) put it in their view to 2030: "Once the large Baby Boom generation begins to decline in number and scale back its occupancy of housing (starting within 10 years) ... the *demographic pressure for price increases and new construction will slacken, and mismatches between housing stock supply and demand will leave substantial portions of the national housing stock subject to increased vacancy, disinvestment, and potential demolition or conversion*" (p. 26). (italics added)

In their fifties, most Boomers became empty nesters. As they age their preferences for neighborhood and community attributes change as well. What are those preferences? Analysis of a survey by the National Association of Home Builders by Myers and Gearin (2001) showed that as people age their preference for smaller homes and smaller lots increases. They found that the preference for townhouses increases from about 9 percent among those aged twenty-four to thirty-five, to 24 percent among those fifty-five and over. This portends a boom in townhouse demand to 2030 and beyond.

Despite having the highest rate of home ownership among all age groups (about 80 percent), when a senior household moves, it is more likely to rent as own, and in any event the house and lot size is reduced.[4] Seniors moving into managed care facilities (independent living, assisted living, and nursing) or moving in with family or friends

will typically sell their homes, using the proceeds plus retirement benefits to help pay costs. Data from the American Housing Survey (US
HUD 2010) show that about 3–5 percent of households sixty-five and
over move each year, but when they do, about sixty percent rent.

A national survey conducted in 2004 for the National Association
of Realtors and Smart Growth America (Belden Russonello & Stewart 2004) included questions on accessibility to certain destinations
within about a fifteen-minute walk. Although respondents aged fifty-
nine and over did not desire walking access to shops and restaurants
as much as younger groups, they ranked higher than any other group
in their preference to live within walking distance of public transit.

Seniors will become significant contributors to the growing "new
urbanism" movement (see Leinberger 2007a; Nelson 2009a). Their
motivation is pragmatic: they want to live in places that are accessible
to key destination such as shopping, services, and medical care.

Consider three key ingredients of the new urbanism that seniors
value:

First there is the ability to walk from home to several destinations.
As they age, seniors often engage in more walking in part because they
have more time (away from raising a family and working) and because
they more readily see its value in personal health. This includes walking to family and friends, community and senior centers, parks, convenience services such as grocery stores and pharmacies, and personal
care. Research on the particular benefits of walking for seniors is sur-
prisingly lacking, though general research on benefits is voluminous
and growing (see Handy et al. 2002). Work by Li et al. (2009) indicates that among people aged fifty to seventy-five better neighborhood
walkability and increased levels of physical activity appear to be associated with maintaining a healthy weight over time.[5]

Second, integrated land uses reduce dependency on single-
occupant vehicle use. This not only advances the ability to walk but
improves the opportunities for being driven to places by family or
friends, or in worst-case situations being able to get from home to
medical care in an emergency (see National Alliance of Public Transportation Advocates 2008). Indeed, up to 60 percent of seniors may be
public transportation-dependent (AARP Public Policy Institute 1997,

15). In many suburban areas, transit is such an option only by increasing density through infill and redevelopment, especially along commercial corridors (Nelson 2006).

Finally, urban housing options are commensurate with life stage needs. In a typical cycle of housing, young people need rental options, young families need starter homes, maturing families need larger homes, empty nesters need small homes, and at advanced ages most people need assisted living or similar arrangements (Lodl et al. 2005). All too often, empty nesters would prefer a smaller home but do not want to sacrifice the neighborhood and community networks they have created; thus, they age in place to maintain them. Unfortunately, communities can not always successfully support families with school-age children and empty nesters; zoning preventing fixed residential options also gets in the way. The new urbanism would result in neighborhoods that allow households of all life stages to have the option of living in them. This includes such affordable housing options as higher density housing and accessory dwelling units in existing homes.

But living in a new urbanism location is not a universal desire among Baby Boomers. We might conclude, based on survey information, that a third to half of all seniors would want the new urbanism, which means half, if not most, may not.

It may very well be that most seniors will choose to live as long as they can in their current home. For some the choice is a negative one, because we know from Myers and Ryu (2008) that many millions of seniors will not be able to sell their homes for lack of buyers, at least at a price seniors are willing to accept. Many other millions would rather live as long as they can where they are. The growing field of "aging-in-place" studies explores reasons for not relocating and options for doing so. Some advantages include sustaining social networks, sharing the home with relatives or others, and avoiding the trauma of moving. Some disadvantages include being far away from medical care or incurring the cost of in-home care, being away from senior-related social services, and stressing the local fiscal base through deferred property tax assessment and/or increased demand for age-related public services. This is an emerging area of research, policy, and practice that needs more in-depth treatment than I can provide here.

## WALKABILITY AND BIKABILITY

I now explore walking and biking preferences for all age groups estimating the extent to which those preferences are met. For this, I use a survey larger than NAR (2011). It is the proprietary survey data set provided by Porter-Novelli, a consumer survey firm.[6] Annually, it conducts a survey tracking a variety of consumer and health behaviors. In its 2003 and 2005 surveys, Porter-Novelli gauged market preferences for a variety of smart growth attributes, including the extent to which people believe it is important or very important to be able to walk or bike to work and shopping. The surveys were quite large, with 5,873 participants in 2003 and 4,943 in 2005. Because Porter-Novelli asked the same questions in those years, the total sample size was 10,816. The survey included two questions asking, on a scale of 1 ("not at all important") to 5 ("very important"), "how personally important is it to you to . . . be able to walk or bike to work . . . or . . . be able to walk or bike to shopping."

The respondents were divided into four age groups: 18–34, 35–54, 55–69, and 70+.[7] The age group 18–34 corresponds to a youthful population that is just staring out in life, building careers (including attending college), and starting families—they are the Gen Y households. Table 2.1 shows the extent to which respondents think it is personally important for them to be able to walk or bike to work, and walk or bike for shopping and other errands. A little less than a quarter of American households believe that walking and biking accessibility is very important. There is not much variation by age, but there is a large variation with respect to income. Twenty-eight and 27 percent of lower income households find walking and biking opportunities to be important, respectively, compared to just 16 percent for the upper income category. At 28 and 29 percent for walking and biking opportunities, respectively, a larger share of single-person households finds these options to be important than larger households (18–22 percent).

These numbers might seem small; after all, more than three-quarters of respondents do not believe that being able to walk or bike to work is important or very important. Also, we know from the National Household Travel Survey that only about 4 percent of all

*Table 2.1* How personally important is it to be able to walk or bike to work and for shopping/errands?

| Demographic group | Important/ very important— work (%) | Important/ very important— shopping and errands (%) |
|---|---|---|
| All | 23 | 22 |
| Age | | |
| 18–34 | 24 | 22 |
| 35–54 | 21 | 20 |
| 55–69 | 23 | 24 |
| 70+ | 24 | 25 |
| Income | | |
| <80% AMI | 28 | 27 |
| 80–120% AMI | 19 | 18 |
| >120% AMI | 16 | 16 |
| Household type | | |
| Single person | 28 | 29 |
| Larger, no children | 22 | 21 |
| Larger, with children | 20 | 18 |

*Source*: Porter-Novelli (2003, 2005).
*Note*: AMI = area median income for the state.

workers actually do walk or bike to work and only about 10 percent walk or bike for shopping or for other errands.

However, if we look at whether working or shopping/errand destinations are within one mile from the trip origins, we see something very different, as shown in table 2.2. Here we see that the share of trips by walking or biking to work or shopping/other errands has increased steadily between 1995 and 2009 (the Porter-Novelli preference survey discussed above was conducted in 2005). When destinations are within a mile, it turns out that about 35 percent and 40 percent of Americans walk and bike to work and for errands, respectively, and the share has increased steadily since 1995.

In 2009, fewer than 3 percent of Americans enjoyed this accessibility. One can only imagine the benefits if only the quarter of Ameri-

*Table* 2.2 Percent of trips by walking or biking to work and for shopping or other errands, 1995–2009.

| Year | *Walk/bike to work* <br> *< 1 mile (%)* | *Walk/bike for shopping/errands* <br> *< 1 Mile (%)* |
|---|---|---|
| 1995 | 25 | 26 |
| 2001 | 34 | 35 |
| 2009 | 37 | 42 |
| Change 1995–2009 | 48 | 62 |

*Source:* Adapted from the National Household Transportation Survey (2011).

cans who want the option to walk or bike to within one mile of work and errand destinations had that option.

The demand for alternatives to highways appears large and may be growing. A 2004 survey, for instance, found that 46 percent of all Americans want to live within walking distance of public transit (Belden Russonello & Stewart 2004). More recent surveys indicate this figure is growing and many now approach 60 percent (Handy et al. 2008). By 2030 the United States will grow to about 363 million people[8] living in about 143 million households.[9] From surveys, we know that at least half of them, about 70 million households, will want to live near transit. We also know that of the nation's 115 million households in 2010, about 43 million or 37 percent of them lived within a ten-minute walk of transit.[10] The implication is that of the nearly 30 million new housing units needed between 2010 and 2030,[11] all of them would need to be built where transit exists or is planned, and even this will not meet all the demand.

## HOUSING DEMAND AND SUPPLY MISMATCH

In recent years, three national studies have reported broad national preference trends for housing by type of housing unit. I use those surveys to estimate the demand for the new urbanism, which is very much at odds with the current supply of housing.

Those surveys are of Americans' preference for housing by major type of housing. They include attached units, including apartments, townhouses, condominiums, multiplexes, and cooperatives, among others; small lot (as defined by each survey); and conventional lots, which would be all other detached options. The surveys include one by me (Nelson 2006), one by RCLCO (2008), and one by the National Association of Realtors (NAR 2011).

Although consensus exists among surveys on what constitutes attached units, such as apartments, condominiums, cooperatives, and townhouses, there is no consensus on what constitutes "small" or "conventional" lots. For instance, the Nelson (2006) survey defined small lots as one-sixth acre (six units per acre). RCLCO's 2008 survey defined small lots as one-quarter acre (four units per acre). The NAR survey (2011) left it up to respondents to self-define what a small lot was. Other surveys implicitly define a small lot as one-eighth acre or smaller (eight or more units per acre) because research shows this size is the minimum detached residential unit density that supports transit use (see Baldassare 2001, 2002).[12]

My 2006 analysis synthesized numerous surveys reported by development interests from the mid-1990s to the early 2000s to estimate the distribution of housing choice options people wanted. I found that among both owners and renters, about 38 percent of Americans wanted attached residential options, 37 percent wanted detached residential units on small lots, and 25 percent wanted what I call conventional lot options. The surveys I reviewed suggested that "small" lots were those under about one-sixth of an acre.

RCLCO (2008) conducted another national survey of prospective buyers in 2007 to understand what Gen X and Gen Y households preferred to buy as opposed to rent. It gave special treatment to Gen Y. Here are some highlights of Gen Y housing and neighborhood preferences reported by RCLCO:[13]

- Overall, for those who were moving, the most interest was for neighborhoods close to urban areas, followed by urban locations.
- Prospective home buyers had a strong preference for walkability.
  - This preference was driven by convenience, connectivity, and a healthy work/life balance to maintain relationships.

- ○ One-third would pay more for housing from which they could walk to shops, work, and entertainment.
- ○ Two-thirds said that living in a walkable community is important.
- ○ More than one-half of Gen Y households would trade lot size for proximity to shopping or to work.
- ○ Among families with children, one-third or more were willing to trade lot size for walkable, diverse communities.
- ○ In the suburbs, the majority of Gen Yers preferred characteristics of urban places, especially walkability.
- Regarding family changes:
  - ○ Seventy percent did not believe they had to move to the suburbs once they have children; and
  - ○ Only half were confident they would need a single-family home once they have children.
- Community and neighborhood needs reflected the following:
  - ○ Diversity was a key ingredient—Gen Y want diversity in housing types, styles, groups of people, and composition.
  - ○ More than half reported that having a community and home designed to meet certain green objectives plays an important role in their purchase or renting decision.

The RCLCO survey of prospective home buyers found that 34 percent preferred to have the option to buy an attached unit, 35 percent wished to have the small-lot option (being one-quarter acre lots or smaller), and the rest, some 31 percent, preferred the conventional-lot option.

The NAR survey (2011) indicated that about 39 percent of Americans want the option to own or rent an attached unit, 37 percent want the small-lot option, and 24 percent prefer the conventional-lot option.

These three, very different approaches to estimating Americans' preferences for housing by type are summarized in table 2.3. Mine, of owners and renters (Nelson 2006), was a synthesis of several housing industry surveys between the mid-1990s and the mid-2000s. The RCLCO (2008) survey was conducted in-house and focused only on prospective home buyers. The NAR (2011) survey included owners

*Table 2.3* Demand and supply of housing by major type

| House type | Nelson demand (2006) | RCLCO demand (2007)[a] | NAR demand (2011) | AHS supply (2009) |
|---|---|---|---|---|
| Attached | 38% | 34% | 39% | 30% |
| Small lot[b] | 37% | 35% | 37% | 20% |
| Conventional lot | 25% | 31% | 24% | 50% |

*Sources:* Nelson 2006; RCLCO 2008 (2007 survey); NAR 2011; American Housing Survey (AHS) for 2009 (US HUD 2010).
[a] Buyer demand only
[b] For Nelson (2006) and AHS (2009), "small lot" indicates under one-sixth acre

and renters and was tailored specifically to explore trade-offs between housing and location choices. What is impressive is that for the most part they say the same thing, that nearly 40 percent of American households want attached residential options, more than a third want small-lot options, and a quarter want conventional-lot options.

What about supply? Data for 2009 from the American Housing Survey (US HUD 2010) indicate that attached housing comprises about 30 percent of the supply, small lots (under one-sixth of an acre) are about 20 percent of the supply, and conventional lots are about half of the supply. Clearly, there is a mismatch between supply of attached, small-lot, and conventional-lot housing compared to demand. This may be one reason why larger homes, especially in distant suburban areas, have lost value disproportionately than other types of housing closer in.[14]

## GEN Y AS THE NEXT BIG MARKET

As I noted at the beginning of this chapter, Gen Y—those born between 1981 and 1995 and numbering about seventy-one million people will dominate the housing market between 2010 and 2030. Their preferences will help to shape the future of housing and urban form. Many millions may choose to replace Boomers in large homes on large lots in the suburbs, but many other millions will want something different.

For instance, Norris (2012) observes that Gen Y will prefer downtowns, suburban centers, and mixed-use neighborhoods with housing options that are close to destinations. The irony, of course, is that Gen Y people mostly grew up in isolated, single-use suburban subdivisions. Norris makes four observations about what Gen Y will look for in homes and neighborhoods, to which I add additional insights.

First, they may want to be connected and not isolated. This is manifest in their use of social media to stay in touch with people. Social media draws people closer together as they text instantly where they are and where they want to meet up with others. Gen Yers may prefer more densely settled areas where they can take full advantage of these social networks.

Second, they may prefer convenience and low maintenance residential living. Norris (2012) observes that Gen Y has little tolerance for spending time on things like driving, caring for yards, or maintaining large homes. They demand the convenience of living close to destinations such as coffee shops, restaurants, and stores that are down the street and not a twenty-minute drive away. Developers of new communities understand this; they design and market their projects as live-work-play communities.

Third, as many Gen Y prefer to be car-independent. The *New York Times* reports that automobile manufacturers are perplexed that many young, prospective car buyers are not that interested in cars.[15] Norris thinks that Gen Yers would rather take a bus, bike, or train than drive; indeed, employers such as Google locate their offices in urban settings near transit or they provide transit.

Fourth, Gen Y values the ability to relocate easily to maximize their economic and social benefits. For many, this means not being tied to a home they may be unable to sell quickly to seize new opportunities. Moreover, unlike prior generations, Gen Y does not trust that home ownership will create investment equity. Thus, many will choose to rent rather than own.

These drivers of residential location choice will not apply to all Gen Y people—maybe just a third of them. But that third, perhaps 10 million households, will reshape our built landscape. In the next chapter, I show population, household, and housing trends (chapter 5) and their implications for reshaping metropolitan America.

# 3

# HOUSEHOLDS AND HOUSING

As America's population is changing, so will its household composition and housing needs. With their buying power and need for space to raise growing families, Baby Boomers dominated the market for new homes from the 1980s through the 2000s. Tens of millions of large homes on large lots were built to meet their needs, and they could afford them. Those days are gone, never to return. Instead, future generations of households and aging Boomers themselves will want something different from what they had in the past. The next generation of households will be more racially and ethnically diverse, earn less income, and have fewer opportunities for home ownership than prior generations.

In this chapter I show that American households and housing needs will be very different in 2030 compared to 2010. The bottom line for American housing between 2010 and 2030 is that the days of hyper demand for large homes on large lots are over.

## HOUSEHOLDS

By estimating the number and future distribution of households by type, we can infer emerging housing needs. A household is defined as a person or group of people living together in one dwelling unit.

## Changing Household Size

Estimating the number of households in 2030 involves estimating the population living in households (as opposed to living in group quarters such as nursing homes, dormitories, and prisons) and dividing it by the projected average household size. Census and commercial vendors such as Woods & Poole Economics, Inc., produce population projections that are nearly accurate over short periods and reasonably accurate over one to two decades. Not so easy is projecting future average household size. The census does not do this, but Woods & Poole Economics does, which I adapt their figures in this book, with permission.

   Projecting future household size is important because it also helps to project housing needs. For instance, it seems everyone was fooled by assuming in 2000 that the average household size would fall from 2.59 then to 2.52 by 2010 (Day 1996); yet it was actually at 2.58, very close to its 2000 level, as illustrated in figure 3.1. This trend is commonly blamed on the Great Recession, which caused many people to double up and forced more children to stay with their parents longer. I will now explore the implications for stabilizing household size.

*Figure 3.1* Average household size by decade, 1900–2010.

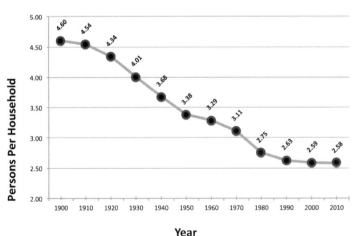

*Source*: US Census data. Figure by J. P. Goates

Starting at 4.60 persons per household in 1900, the average household size in the United States fell steadily to 2.59 in 2000.[1]

In 1950, when the average household size was 3.38,[2] one million people would occupy about 297,000 housing units. Those same one million people in 2000, when the average household size was 2.59, would occupy 386,000 housing units—30 percent more. Indeed, declining household size drove much of America's suburbanization between 1950 and 2000. For the nation as a whole, while population grew by 85 percent between 1950 and 2000, its occupied housing stock rose by 140 percent because average household size fell from 3.38 to 2.59. Had the household size remained at the 1950 level, the inventory of occupied units would have been a bit more than 80 million units and not the roughly 105 million units there were; this is a difference of about 25 million units.

Indeed, some cities were losing population and making headlines every decade as population fell but the number of housing units actually increased. Washington, DC, for instance, saw its population fall from more than 800,000 to about 572,000 between 1925 and 2000. Yet, its occupied housing stock rose from about 220,000 to more than 250,000 units because average household size fell from 2.72 to 2.16.[3] The consequence is that, because of declining household size, Washington, DC, has more housing units now than ever before, even though its population is about a third of its height.

The trend of declining average household size has stopped and may even be reversing, meaning that housing growth will be more a function of population growth only and not decreasing household size. As noted earlier, in 2000, the average household size was projected to fall from 2.59 persons to 2.52 by 2010. This alone would have increased new housing demand by three million homes. But household size in 2010 turned out to be 2.58 persons. To the extent that the market assumed smaller household size in 2010 than in 2000, housing production exceeded demand. Reasons for the stabilization of household size are not only related to the Great Recession, as I will show next.

Over the next decade, household size will not change much from 2000 or 2010 levels. A key reason is the rise of the multigenerational household. These are households that include two generations with parents (or in-laws) and adult children aged twenty-five and older; three generations: parents (or in-laws), adult children (and spouse), and grandchildren; "skipped" generation with grandparents and grandchildren, without parents (including stepchildren); or more than three generations (Pew Research Center 2010: 2).

Multigenerational households have been common throughout the history of the United States. In 1900, about 24 percent of Americans lived in them, rising to about a quarter by the end of the Great Depression. The share of Americans living in these households fell steadily from 1940 to 1980, hitting a low of about 12 percent. Since then, the share of Americans living in multigenerational households has risen steadily, almost in a straight line, to 16 percent in 2008. (See figure 3.2 for trends.)

According to Taylor et al. (2010), the growth in multigenerational households since 1980 is attributable partly to demographic and cultural shifts, including the rising share of immigrants in the population and the rising median age of the first marriage of adults. The trend since 1980 has affected adults of all ages, especially the elderly and the young. By 2010, about one in five adults aged twenty-five to thirty-

*Figure 3.2* Percent population living in multigenerational households, 1900–2008.

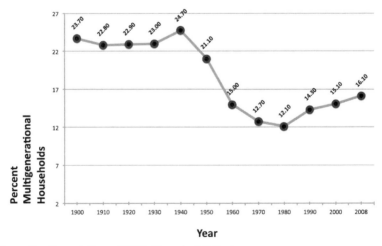

*Source*: Pew Research Center (2010). Figure by J. P. Goates

four lived in a multigenerational household and so did one in five adults aged sixty-five and older. Kreider and Ellis (2011) observe that the increase in twenty-five to thirty-four year-olds living in their parents' home began before the Great Recession and has continued beyond it.

This trend affects housing demand. Consider that in 2004 and 2005, the United States achieved its highest home ownership rate since that figure has been collected—about 69 percent. It did so through creative mortgage financing that waived normal underwriting requirements and through very low "teaser" adjustable rate mortgages.[4] Where the sustainable level of home construction during the 2000s was around 1.5 million homes per year (McIlwain 2009), the mid-2000s saw more than two million units built annually. One would think that easy mortgages combined with a glut of housing would reduce average household size. Yet average household size was 2.59 for 2000 and very nearly the same, 2.58, in 2010.[5] One reason household size did not fall appreciably during the 2000s may have been the steady rise of multigenerational households.

My interpretation of the trends indicates that by 2030 about 20 percent (or more) of Americans may be living in multigenerational households. Nonetheless, as the Boomers age and lose their partners, average household size will begin to fall gradually after 2020. By 2030, average household size will be 2.53, about what was projected for 2010.

*Households by Type*

Over its history, the United States has been a nation dominated by youth. The Baby Boom was the end of America's youth movement. As we saw in chapter 1, the nation's population is aging. Between 2010 and 2030, the share of people over sixty-five will increase from 13 percent to 19 percent of the population, an unprecedented shift. Equally unprecedented is that the share of population under eighteen will have fallen from 34 percent in 1970 to 23 percent in 2030.

But population changes tell only part of the story. Although population change between 2010 and 2030 will be dramatic, the change in the distribution of households by type will be even more so.

For instance, in 2010, about 30 percent of all households had children living in them—down from about half in 1960. I estimate that by 2030, households with children will fall to about 27 percent of all households;[6] households without children will thus increase from 70 percent to 73 percent. A key reason is that Boomers, who dominated family formations from the 1980s through the 2000s, will be empty-nesting and losing partners. Gen X (born between 1965 and 1980) was the smallest since World War II and had negligible effects on housing demand, and they, too, are beginning to empty-nest. Gen Y only began family formations in large numbers in the early 2010s and is more likely to remain single and defer family formation to later years than earlier generations. Given these trends, the nature of future housing demand will be vastly different from the past in ways that I will now explore.

The United States will add about 26.3 million households, and households with children will account for only 3.5 million of that change, or about 13 percent of new households (see table 3.1). Households without children will account for about 87 percent of the change in households by type. More than half, 53 percent of the growth in households, will be among single persons—key reasons being Boomers who lose their partners and the emergence of Millennials, who will be mostly in their twenties in 2030. The bottom line is that a new reality has emerged: the future of American planning and public policy will be geared to meeting the needs of households without children, with half of the new market being single-person households. Yet, our planning, zoning, and development codes remain substantially rooted in a reality that no longer exists—that of mass family- and child-oriented markets. We may not be revising our planning tools fast enough to anticipate the needs of a society that is already very different from the twentieth century and that will be even more different as the twenty-first century unfolds.

*Households by Age Group*

As the Boomers age their household size falls, thus increasing their demand for housing; and because they are the largest population group,

*Table 3.1* Households by type, 2010–2030 (figures in thousands).

| Measure | Households 2010 | Households 2030 | Household Change (2010–2030) | Percent Change (2010–2030, %) | Share of Change (%) |
|---|---|---|---|---|---|
| Total households | 116,945 | 143,232 | 26,287 | 22 | |
| HHs with children | 34,814 | 38,358 | 3,544 | 10 | 13 |
| HHs without children | 82,131 | 104,874 | 22,743 | 28 | 87 |
| *Single-person HHs* | *31,264* | *45,081* | *13,817* | *44* | *53* |

*Note:* Percentages may not sum due to rounding.

their emerging demand for empty-nest/downsized, post–sixty-five housing will dominate the market, just as their needs have through all stages of their life. As Boomers turn sixty-five between 2011 and 2029, their average household size will have shrunk from their peak of about 3.40 (for householders aged thirty-five to thirty-nine) to 1.58 for those Boomers born before 1955—less than half.

This is only part of the story. The peak period of buying the largest homes in a household's life cycle is between the ages of thirty-five and sixty-four. This is when households have the motive in terms of growing families and housing space needs, the means in terms of income (often dual incomes), and opportunity in having access to inexpensive housing built on cheap land away from urban and suburban centers. I call this the "triple storm" of housing demand because it is composed of the motive to buy ever larger homes to support growing households, the means in terms of income to buy those homes, and the opportunity to buy homes at attractive prices mostly in the suburbs. Consider income. The period between 1993 and 2007 saw the median household income increase to unprecedented levels, as seen in figure 3.3. Median household income broke $50,000 in 1997 and was $52,823 ten years later in 2007. Even during the 2001 recession real median household incomes remained above $50,000.

*Figure 3.3* Median household income from 1975 through 2010 in constant 2010 dollars.

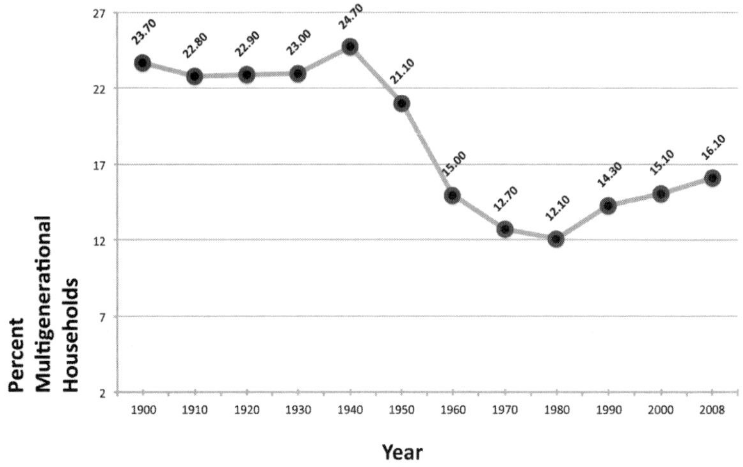

*Source*: US Census data. Figure by J. P. Goates

The triple storm of motive-means-opportunity reached its zenith during the period 1980 to 2010. Figure 3.4 illustrates the five-year over five-year net change in the share of householders aged thirty-five to sixty-four compared to those under thirty-five and sixty-five or older. Over the period 1980–1985 through 2005–2010, this peak-consumption age group accounted for nearly 80 percent of the total demand for housing, peaking at 100 percent during the period 1995–2000.

Table 3.2 illustrates this further. Using data from the American Housing Survey for 1989 and 2009, we see that of the more than twenty-four million residential units built during this period, about 85 percent, were detached single-family homes (including mobile homes). More than a quarter of them had twenty-five hundred or more square feet of living space. Even more remarkable is that more than one-third of all new residential units and 42 percent of all new detached homes were built on lots of one-half to ten acres of land during this period.

But the triple storms have passed. In tables 3.3 and 3.4, I compare housing demand by major household age group for equal twenty-year

*Figure 3.4* Five-year change in share of householders aged thirty-five to sixty-four relative to change in all households, 1970–1975 to 2005–2010.

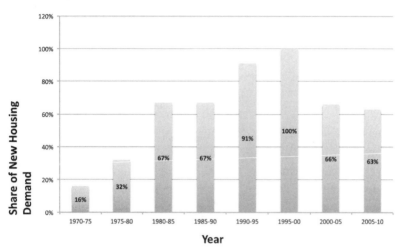

*Note:* For the five-year period 1980–1985, 67 percent of the net change in total households between the five-year period 1975–1980 and 1980–1985 was attributable to the growth in the number of householders aged thirty-five to sixty-four.
*Source:* US Census data. Figure by J. P. Goates

*Table 3.2* Change in housing unit features, 1989–2009 (figures in thousands).

| Feature | 1989 | 2009 | Change (1989–2009) | Change (1989–2009, %) | Change share (1989–2009, %) | Detached unit change share (1989–2009, %) |
|---|---|---|---|---|---|---|
| Total | 105,651 | 130,112 | 24,461 | 23 | | |
| Detached | 70,495 | 91,241 | 20,746 | 29 | 85 | |
| Homes 2,500 square feet and over | 12,649 | 19,297 | 6,648 | 53 | 27 | 32 |
| Lots 0.5 to 10 acres | 24,887 | 33,568 | 8,681 | 35 | 35 | 42 |

*Note:* Figures may not sum due to rounding.
*Source:* American Housing Survey.

periods, 1990 to 2010 (table 3.3) and 2010 to 2030 (table 3.4). Those groups include starter-home households where the householder is less than thirty-five years old, households where the householders are between thirty-five and sixty-four years old who are in their peak demand for housing space (who have the motivation, the monetary means, and the opportunity), and empty-nesting/downsizing households where the householder is sixty-five years of age or older. Table 3.3 shows that between 1990 and 2010, the number of starter-home households fell by about two million, while the number of households in the peak demand for housing grew by about twenty million, accounting for 83 percent of the entire demand for new housing. Empty-nesting/downsizing households accounted for the remaining 17 percent of the new demand. As children, Boomers became America's true first-generation suburbanites, and as they raised their own families they shaped suburbs even more. But that will change as Boomers age.

The trend between 2010 and 2030 will be equally dramatic, as illustrated in table 3.4. Starter households will account for 10 percent of the share of housing change but households in their peak housing

*Table 3.3* Share of growth in householders by age category, 1990–2010 (figures in thousands).

| Householder age | Households, 1990 | Households, 2010 | Household change (1990–2010) | Percent change (1990–2010, %) | Share of growth (1990–2010, %) |
|---|---|---|---|---|---|
| Total | 92,315 | 116,944 | 24,629 | 27 | |
| < 35 (Starter units) | 25,258 | 23,406 | (1,852) | –7 | |
| 35–64 (Peak space demand) | 47,148 | 67,670 | 20,522 | 44 | 77 |
| 65+ (Empty-nesting/downsizing) | 19,909 | 25,868 | 5,959 | 30 | 23 |

*Note:* Figures may not sum due to rounding.
*Source:* US Census.

*Table 3.4* Change and share of growth in householders by age category, 2010–2030 (figures in thousands.)

| Householder age | Households, 2010 | Households, 2030 | Household change (2010–2030) | Percent change (2010–2030, %) | Share of growth (2010–2030, %) |
|---|---|---|---|---|---|
| Total | 116,944 | 143,232 | 26,288 | 22 | |
| < 35 (Starter units) | 23,406 | 26,074 | 2,668 | 11 | 10 |
| 35–64 (Peak space demand) | 67,670 | 71,772 | 4,102 | 6 | 16 |
| 65+ (Empty-nesting/downsizing) | 25,868 | 45,385 | 19,517 | 75 | 74 |

*Note:* Figures may not sum due to rounding.
*Source:* US Census for 2010 and estimates for 2030.

consumption stage of life will account for another 16 percent or just one-fifth the demand share seen during 1990 and 2000. Empty-nesting/downsizing households will command 74 percent of the total share of change in housing demand. The reason is that Boomers, who drove the demand for detached homes on large lots during the 1980s through 2000s, have raised their children, are retiring, and will seek different living accommodations.[7] Indeed, aging Boomers may attempt to sell millions more large homes on large lots over the next few decades than the market can absorb, especially in slow-growing or stagnating metropolitan areas. The era of conventional-lot suburban homes meeting the needs of Baby Boom parents and the Boomers themselves would seem to be over. However, there is another trend: the rise of a more racially and ethnically diverse population.

## Households by Race/Ethnicity

Sometime in the 2040s, the United States will become a nation mostly of minorities, though white households will be in the plurality. Along the way, between 2010 and 2030, America's growing diversity will change the face of its housing market. In many regions and metropolitan areas, minority households will account for all or nearly all the demand for new family-based housing, yet fewer of them will be able to afford to buy those homes than child-oriented households of the past. The aging Boomers will also demand housing and neighborhoods more suitable to them than the homes many millions live in now. This section estimates the share of change in household growth based on major minority groups.

In the mid-2000s, less than half of the nation's population growth was among the white population, who own homes at a much higher rate than the national average. Figure 3.5 shows the home ownership rate among selected racial and ethnic groups. Over the decade of the 2000s, there was little change in the home ownership rates among these groups. As America's households become more diverse to 2030, the aggregate home-ownership rate will surely fall, unless efforts

*Figure 3.5* Home ownership rates among selected racial/ethnic groups, 2000–2010.

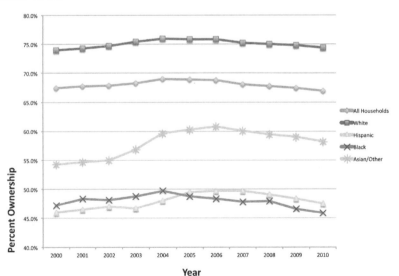

*Source*: Data from Joint Center for Housing Study (2011), Source: Current Population Survey/ Housing Vacancy Survey, Series H-111. Figure by J. P. Goates

are made to loosen underwriting requirements, reduce down payments, further incentivize ownership, and especially invest in the education minority children need to earn incomes that support home ownership.

We know from chapter 1 that minorities will comprise about 86 percent of the total change in population from 2010 to 2030. However, because minority households are larger while aging Baby Boomer households are smaller, minorities will account for about 75 percent of the change in households. In contrast, white households will grow by only 7 percent yet their share of total household growth will be 25 percent. The reason is that as white Boomers become seniors, their household size shrinks by up to half from just two decades earlier. Nonetheless, minority household growth will dominate this period.

## HOUSING

The members of a households need a place to live, so in this section I estimate housing needs to 2030. My estimate will account for vacant, seasonal, and other units not permanently occupied. Because housing units do not last forever—though they can survive a long time, as will be seen—my calculations include a replacement factor.

### Total Housing Units Needed by 2030

An estimate of the number of vacant, seasonal, transitional, and other units usually requires an analysis of local market characteristics. For instance, a market with too many vacant housing units could drive prices down, thereby dampening new construction, while a market with too few vacant units can drive prices up, thereby accelerating construction. The objective is to find the locally efficient vacancy rate factor considering growth rates; market trends; characteristics of the current housing stock, especially its age and condition; and market demand for housing niches that have changed (see Nelson 2004). Similar exercises are needed to estimate local demand for seasonal, transitional, and other units. These analyses help craft reasonably accurate estimates of future needs, especially for smaller communities, but that is not the purpose of this book.

Given these caveats, I estimate the number of all housing units per capita from the 2000 census and multiply that coefficient by the population projected for 2030. I would prefer to use the 2010 census, but it will show artificially high multipliers because of the excessive construction of the 2000s. The approach I use elegantly considers vacant and seasonal homes by its nature because all housing units are included, not just occupied ones or ones by type or tenancy (owner versus renter). It assumes that household size will not change, at least by much, but because household size appears to have stabilized anyway, this should be reasonable. The approach also assumes no dramatic change in the popularity of seasonal homes—those areas that are already attractive for second homes will continue to be such and few new areas will emerge. While once thought of as a booming market as the Baby Boomers turn sixty-five between 2011 and 2029 (Zhu et al. 2001), the seasonal/second home market picture has been tempered.[8]

*Lost and Replaced Housing*

Houses burn down, blow down, flood, shake to the ground, make way for "monster" homes or new developments, and in many other ways are eliminated from the housing stock. The extent to which housing units will be lost over time needs to be addressed. What is the appropriate assumption? I have previously written (Nelson 2004) that, nationally, housing is lost at a rate of about 0.58 percent per year compounded. By removing mobile homes from the analysis, Pitken and Myers (2008) found the average annual rate of loss is about 0.50 percent. I use their figure as the overall national control. For individual states and core-based statistical areas, I use the local growth rate as a proportion to the national growth rate to estimate housing units that need to be replaced. Thus, areas growing faster than the national average will need to replace homes at a faster rate than slower growing ones.

Table 3.5 reports the total number of housing units needed for the nation and census regions and divisions (see www.ReshapeMetro America.org for more details). It suggests several key findings:

- Using my method of estimating demand for housing in 2010, I show that the nation had about 4.2 million more units than the market demanded.[9] These units are available to meet future housing needs.
- Between 2010 and 2030, the nation will need to add about 22.7 million homes to its inventory or about 1.3 million annually.
- During this period, another 10.9 million units will need to be built to replace units existing in 2010 that will be removed from the inventory.
- Total new housing construction for the nation over the period 2010 to 2030 comes to about 36.7 million units, or about 1.8 million units per year. Given the excess supply in 2010 and that several hundred thousand units were built annually during the early 2010s, this level may not be reached until the later 2020s.

*Housing Tenure*

Since 1950, when America's home ownership rate was 55 percent, ownership has dominated over renting. In 1960, the ownership rate rose to 61.9 percent and then 62.9 percent in 1970. The ownership rate continued to grow to 64.4 percent in 1980, but remained about the same in 1990 (the decade started and ended with recessions), 64.2 percent. The ownership rate accelerated to 66.2 percent in 2000[10] and peaked at 69 percent in 2004[11] before falling to 65.1 percent in 2010.

The 1980s, the decade of the 2000s was the first since 1950 to see a significant decline in home ownership rate, falling from 66.2 percent to 65.1 percent. As I discussed earlier, there are many reasons for this, such as the home purchase exigencies of the early to mid-2000s, in which households that would not have otherwise qualified for mortgages were lured into them anyway, followed by the crash of the real estate market.[12] Future ownership rates are likely to fall for other reasons.

Home ownership depends on incomes large enough to afford mortgages, and incomes depend mostly on education to compete in the workforce. If public investments in minority education were effective, we should see the gap in test scores between whites and minorities fall; indeed, by eliminating the gap, the differences among ownership

Table 3.5 Housing construction needs for the nation, and census regions and divisions, 2010-2030 (figures in thousands)

| Geographic area | Housing units existing 2010 | Housing units supported 2010 | Difference between supply and demand 2010 | Housing units needed, 2030 | Net change to housing stock (2010-2030) | Housing units replaced (2010-2030) | Total housing units built (2010-2030) | Housing built as share of housing in 2010 (%) |
|---|---|---|---|---|---|---|---|---|
| United States | 131,705 | 127,543 | (4,162) | 157,508 | 25,803 | 10,942 | 36,745 | 28 |
| *Census regions* | | | | | | | | |
| Northeast | 23,648 | 22,825 | (823) | 25,777 | 2,130 | 1,771 | 3,901 | 16 |
| Midwest | 29,484 | 27,614 | (1,870) | 32,226 | 2,742 | 2,244 | 4,986 | 17 |
| South | 49,981 | 47,358 | (2,622) | 63,486 | 13,505 | 4,426 | 17,930 | 36 |
| West | 28,593 | 29,746 | 1,153 | 36,019 | 7,427 | 2,500 | 9,927 | 35 |
| *Census divisions* | | | | | | | | |
| New England | 6,419 | 5,961 | (458) | 7,172 | 754 | 495 | 1,249 | 19 |
| Mid Atlantic | 17,229 | 16,864 | (365) | 18,605 | 1,376 | 1,276 | 2,653 | 15 |
| East North Central | 20,376 | 19,146 | (1,230) | 21,823 | 1,447 | 1,525 | 2,972 | 15 |
| West North Central | 9,107 | 8,467 | (640) | 10,402 | 1,295 | 719 | 2,014 | 22 |
| South Atlantic | 26,872 | 24,706 | (2,166) | 34,029 | 7,157 | 2,394 | 9,552 | 36 |
| East South Central | 8,186 | 7,610 | (576) | 9,743 | 1,557 | 675 | 2,233 | 27 |
| West South Central | 14,923 | 15,042 | 119 | 19,713 | 4,790 | 1,356 | 6,146 | 41 |
| Mountain | 9,525 | 9,127 | (398) | 12,573 | 3,048 | 883 | 3,931 | 41 |
| Pacific | 19,068 | 20,619. | 1,551 | 23,447 | 4,379 | 1,617 | 5,996 | 31 |

*Note:* Figures may not sum due to rounding.
*Source:* Census for 2010 and estimates for 2030.

rates of racial/ethnic groups could disappear. This is not happening. The National Center for Educational Statistics (2009, 2011) shows that since the mid-1990s, the standardized test score gap among whites, blacks, and Hispanics has not changed appreciably over the past decade. The result for the future is lower incomes and higher unemployment rates. This will also affect long-term national home-ownership rates.

To estimate the home-ownership rate in 2030, I take the rates for 2010 by racial/ethnic group and apply them to households in 2030 based on minority status. This approach may overstate the demand for owner-occupied homes given the trends noted in chapter 1. I thus estimate the national home-ownership rate will be about 63.1 percent in 2030,[13] down from 65.1 percent in 2010, which is also down from 66.2 percent in 2000. At this rate, nearly half of all new dwelling units built between 2010 and 2030 will need to be for renters; existing owner-occupied units will need to be converted into rentals; or owners will rent portions of their homes to others, assuming local zoning codes and home owner associations allow this. These figures are reported in table 3.6.

What does all this mean for America's housing markets?

## IMPLICATIONS

In chapter 2, I showed that housing preferences are changing in America. In this chapter, I showed that the very population group that drove America's suburbanization over the past several decades—mostly white households with means, has moved on. Demand for suburban, low-density, owner-occupied housing has diminished. The changing profile of the American home buyer will have important implications for the type of housing stock that needs to be built to 2030. Preference surveys show there is more demand for attached and small-lot housing than there is supply. Housing finance, household income, and demographic trends suggest that this mismatch may widen. The oversupply by tens of millions of homes on conventional lots, mostly in the suburban fringe and exurbs is probably not going away and

Table 3.6 Housing tenure demand for the nation and census regions and divisions, 2010–2030 (figures in thousands of units).

| Geographic area | Homeowners, 2010 | Ownership rate, 2010 (%) | Homeowners, 2030 | Ownership rate, 2030 (%) | Change in homeowners (2010–2030) | Change in renters (2010–2030) | Total change in households (2010–2030) | Renter share of change (2010–2030, %) |
|---|---|---|---|---|---|---|---|---|
| United States | 76,133 | 65.1 | 89,691 | 63.1 | 13,558 | 12,728 | 26,287 | 48 |
| *Census regions* | | | | | | | | |
| Northeast | 13,213 | 62.2 | 13,688 | 58.3 | 475 | 1,708 | 2,182 | 78 |
| Midwest | 18,161 | 69.2 | 19,725 | 66.9 | 1,564 | 1,727 | 3,290 | 52 |
| South | 29,178 | 66.7 | 36,873 | 64.5 | 7,695 | 5,706 | 13,401 | 43 |
| West | 15,580 | 60.5 | 19,406 | 58.4 | 3,825 | 3,588 | 7,413 | 48 |
| *Census divisions* | | | | | | | | |
| New England | 3,714 | 65.5 | 3,971 | 61.8 | 258 | 496 | 753 | 66 |
| Mid Atlantic | 9,500 | 61.0 | 9,717 | 57.0 | 217 | 1,212 | 1,429 | 85 |
| East North Central | 12,473 | 68.9 | 13,316 | 66.5 | 843 | 1,100 | 1,943 | 57 |
| West North Central | 5,689 | 69.9 | 6,409 | 67.6 | 720 | 627 | 1,347 | 47 |
| South Atlantic | 15,569 | 67.1 | 19,718 | 64.7 | 4,149 | 3,125 | 7,274 | 43 |
| East South Central | 4,979 | 68.9 | 5,912 | 67.3 | 933 | 651 | 1,585 | 41 |
| West South Central | 8,630 | 64.8 | 11,243 | 62.9 | 2,613 | 1,930 | 4,542 | 42 |
| Mountain | 5,475 | 66.2 | 7,249 | 64.3 | 1,774 | 1,243 | 3,017 | 41 |
| Pacific | 10,106 | 57.8 | 12,157 | 55.6 | 2,051 | 2,345 | 4,396 | 53 |

Note: Percentages may not sum due to rounding.

could become a source of affordable housing for millions of households—including as rentals. If action is not taken to re-imagine these areas, the oversupply of homes in suburban fringe and exurban locations may lead to what Leinberger (2008)[14] calls the "next slum." Indeed, an entire industry has arisen in recent years in which foreclosed homes are acquired[15] at a fraction of the original purchase price. The investors then rent the home out, sometimes to the foreclosed party.[16]

In instances in which owners' homes have become too large for them, but have lost too much equity to sell, they could rent out a portion of the home. This rented portion could be in the main part of the house or an accessory dwelling unit (ADU), also known as a "granny flat" or "mother-in-law suite." Unfortunately, ADUs are not allowed in most American suburban communities, and even where they are, home owner associations may prevent this.[17] The market solution is to create informal ADU units anyway—a form of squatter housing American style.[18]

"McMansions" and other large homes offer opportunities for the rental of a room or rooms. I estimate that about six million McMansions were built between the early 1980s and the late 2000s[19] during the triple storm period of Boomer housing demand (see chapter 2). McMansions can be characterized as having at least three thousand square feet, often with as many or more bathrooms than bedrooms, large social gathering places ("great" rooms), often two (or more) master bedroom suites, a secondary kitchen (or at least the option), and large garages with accompanying parking pads in front of them. In many ways, McMansions are prebuilt for multifamily housing—and may be used as such increasingly,[20] if not illegal or in violation of home owner associations.

For the most part, planners and public decision makers do not comprehend the magnitude of changes that will occur in the housing market to 2030. By the time market realities become evident, many options may have been foreclosed. The challenge is to communicate not only the imminence of important changes but how to start framing new strategies to meet new, and very different, market realities.

# 4

# SPACE NEEDS FOR JOBS

As America's housing market will be transformed, so will its non-residential spaces such as offices and shopping—maybe more than some might think. In most urbanized areas, nonresidential space accounts for a third or more of the built environment (excluding rights-of-way and other public spaces) and often accounts for half or more of the taxable value. It is also prone to more rapid depreciation, potential blight, and renewal than residential development.

In this chapter, I present two kinds of projections. The first is for "space-occupying" jobs. Office workers, retailers, teachers, hotel workers, and the like work within enclosed spaces. (In box 4.1 I show the North American Industry Classification System (NAICS) breakdown of jobs that require significant amounts of enclosed spaces. These space-occupying jobs will be in enclosed nonresidential spaces, which I address in the second set of projections in this chapter. People working in agriculture, forestry, fishing, mining, or construction typically do not occupy stationary enclosed spaces and are thus not addressed here.

## SPACE-OCCUPYING EMPLOYMENT PROJECTIONS

Unfortunately, since the 1980s, no federal agency has projected employment over the long term and few commercial services do. Fortunately, Woods & Poole Economics has been making these kinds of projections for decades, and I use their projections with permission.

## BOX 4.1
### Economic Sectors Subtaintially Requires Enclosed Spaces

Allocation of jobs into broad land use categories per the North American Industry Classification System

**Industrial group**
>   Utilities (NAICS 22)
>   Manufacturing (NAICS 31–33)
>   Wholesale trade (NAICS 42)
>   Transportation and warehousing (NAICS 48–49)

**Retail trade and lodging group**
>   Retail trade (NAICS sector 44)
>   Accommodation and food service (NAICS 72)

**Office group**
>   Information (NAICS 51)
>   Finance and insurance (NAICS 52)
>   Real estate and rental and leasing (NAICS 53)
>   Professional and technical services (NAICS 54)
>   Management of companies and enterprises (NAICS 55)
>   Administrative and support services, and waste management (NAICS 56)
>   Other services, except public administration (NAICS 81)
>   Public administration—federal civilian, state, and local (NAICS 92)

**Institutional group**
>   Educational services (NAICS 61)
>   Health care and social assistance (NAICS 62)
>   Arts, entertainment, and recreation (NAICS 71)

Woods & Poole reports jobs based on the US Bureau of Economic Analysis (BEA) definition of a job. This could be a full-time or part-time job and working in an organization or being self-employed. The same person could hold multiple jobs. In contrast, the Census Bureau's County Business Patterns reports only the number of jobs claimed by companies with federal employment identification numbers principally for social security and unemployment purposes. Like Woods & Poole, I use the BEA definition because it is the most expansive.

Overall employment trends tend to follow population trends: growing areas add more jobs while declining ones shed them, but there are qualifications. For instance, although the nation's population will grow by about 20 percent between 2010 and 2030, jobs will increase by about 30 percent. Part of this is recovering the jobs lost during the recession of the late 2000s, but part of it follows the national trend toward larger shares of the population working part time and/or in multiple jobs. Thus, although the Northeast and Midwest will grow by just 9 and 10 percent in population, respectively, jobs will increase at about 2.5 times that rate. Table 4.1 shows total employment trends in 2010, projected to 2030. For a breakdown of total trends by state or the space-occupying trends to 2030 for each major category of land use, see www.ReshapeMetroAmerica.org.

Industrial job growth will lag behind population and overall employment growth, adding less than 7 percent to the group. The retail and lodging and office groups will grow at about the overall rate of total job growth. Institutions, however, will grow by about 49 percent over the period 2010 to 2030. The main reason is health care and social services that will add jobs to meet the needs of the growing senior population.

Estimating employment-based space needs can be complex and fraught with uncertainties about the influence of technology on how space is used in the future. Working at home, telecommuting, office "hotelling"—wherein workers never have an assigned work area but use space when needed based on the task and the need to be in an office—and Internet retailing are often viewed as factors that may reduce the future need for nonresidential space.

*Table 4.1* Total space-occupying employment for the nation and census regions and divisions *(figures in thousands.)*

| Geographic area | Total employment, 2010 | Total employment, 2030 | Total employment change (2010–2030) | Percent employment change (2010–2030, %) |
|---|---|---|---|---|
| United States | 157,249 | 205,447 | 48,198 | 31 |
| *Census regions* | | | | |
| Northeast | 28,305 | 35,604 | 7,299 | 26 |
| Midwest | 31,227 | 39,475 | 8,248 | 26 |
| South | 61,568 | 83,316 | 21,748 | 35 |
| West | 35,385 | 46,018 | 10,632 | 30 |
| *Census divisions* | | | | |
| New England | 14,250 | 18,177 | 3,926 | 28 |
| Mid Atlantic | 14,054 | 17,427 | 3,373 | 24 |
| East North Central | 17,681 | 21,716 | 4,035 | 23 |
| West North Central | 13,546 | 17,758 | 4,212 | 31 |
| South Atlantic | 27,548 | 37,283 | 9,736 | 35 |
| East South Central | 13,620 | 18,486 | 4,866 | 36 |
| West South Central | 20,400 | 27,547 | 7,147 | 35 |
| Mountain | 16,804 | 21,573 | 4,770 | 28 |
| Pacific | 18,582 | 24,444 | 5,863 | 32 |

*Note:* Percentages may not sum due to rounding. For details, see www.ReshapeMetroAmerica .org.
*Source:* Adapted from Woods & Poole Economics, Inc. (2011).

Whether these factors increase the efficiency with which space is used and result in less space needed in the future is uncertain. For example, only a very small share of workers work at home, despite its growing prevalence. In 1990, people working at home accounted for 3.0 percent of all workers, and in 2000 they were just 3.3 percent. Telecommuting does not necessarily reduce office space needs because telecommuters may work from home part of a day or some days of the week then work in the office. Office hotelling applies only to workers who travel and need places to function on the road, but does this mean they need less space than if working in a permanent office or cubicle? Or does it mean they require more space to meet their office needs when aggregated across several hotelling locations? Internet retailing is growing but may plateau because people tend to prefer the tactile and social aspects of shopping. A decade of advances in telecommuting, office use, and retailing technologies has not reduced overall nonresidential space needs. In fact the trend seems to be for increasing square feet per person. Total nonindustrial space in the United States averaged 233 square feet per person in 1992 and 246 square feet per person in 2003.[1]

## TRENDS THAT COULD REDUCE NONRESIDENTIAL SPACE NEEDS BUT WON'T, AT LEAST MUCH

There are three trends that may reduce the demand for nonresidential spaces, though I conclude that their overall effect will not be substantial. They are (1) working at home and teleworking, (2) shrinking office spaces, and (3) reduced retail space demand because of Internet shopping.

### Working at Home and Teleworking

People working at home come in two broad flavors: those who are self-employed and those who are employees. If the share of workers in either or both modes increases, the demand for nonresidential space will decrease. Or will it?

The ever changing economy creates new opportunities for individuals to become their own bosses. Low-cost yet high-end personal computers, e-mail, the Internet and cloud storage of data, front-door pickup and delivery of goods, and other advances have made it very easy for anyone to run a business out of the home, and many millions do. The Great Recession, leading to millions of people being laid off, including many with advanced degrees, could accelerate any trend toward working at home. Still, the evidence does not seem to warrant an assumption that this will happen to an extent that could reduce non-residential space needs substantially.

Teleworkers (also called telecommuters) are quite different. Generally, they are people employed by companies who do some of their work at home. But there is debate on who actually is a true teleworker (Mohktarian et al. 2005). For instance, a common definition of telecommuting has a worker working from home as little as one day per month. Based on this measure, there were about sixteen million teleworkers in both 2000 and 2006. Although the number did not change, the share of teleworkers fell from about 9.7 percent to about 9.1 percent.[2] This is hardly a large number, especially since the other twenty-some days of the month would be spent at the primary workplace.

One reason for teleworking is to overcome the distance between home and work. Indeed, teleworkers typically have much longer commutes than others. In 2001 their average one-way distance to work was 17.4 miles, compared to 12.1 for all workers.[3] As the separation between home and work is reduced, so is the incidence of teleworking.

In a sense, the only real advantage of teleworking is to give long-distance commuters some relief. Given a choice, employers prefer to have workers in the office. As the US Government Accountability Office noted:[4]

- Teleworkers can compromise a firm's support infrastructure because they cannot easily give their computers to information technology support when problems arise;
- Managers worry about uncertainty regarding teleworking and state tax laws, especially if employees commute across state lines; and
- Managers are concerned about workplace health and safety laws, wage and hour laws, and workers' compensation when the workplace is at the home.

A major promise of teleworking is productivity gains because workers are not susceptible to office distractions. Yet, teleworker productivity often falls during the first few weeks because of isolation from the primary work group at the office, not to mention domestic distractions. Productivity also falls because of insufficient office-to-home tools to support collaboration; indeed, work team productivity can erode because isolation can lead to work group disintegration. The outcome can be lower morale of both the office- and home-based workers.[5] Teleworking especially compromises domestic space because it is used for both work and family matters, thus complicating family interaction. For companies, teleworking can challenge resource allocation decisions, especially during downturns. The myth is that teleworking reduces costs. Teleworkers can actually cost more than their office-based colleagues.[6]

On balance, it seems that an important element of the attractiveness of teleworking is simply to avoid commuting time and cost. If America is reshaped to reduce the distance between working and home, teleworking may also be reduced. Still, the share of workers teleworking has been and remains small, with the greatest share of teleworkers still working in the primary office location the vast majority of the time. I do not see teleworking increasing much, if at all, and I do not expect it to reduce nonresidential work space by much, if at all.

*Shrinking Office Spaces*

Some analysts think that the average space per office worker will fall substantially. For decades, the rule of thumb has about 250 square feet of occupied space per office worker or about 300–325 square feet, including support space and vacancies (Nelson 2004). Some suggest that technology may reduce occupied space by 100 square feet or more.[7] Less space per worker means less construction of new or rehabilitated office buildings. CoreNet Global, for instance, predicts that in 2017 the average office worker will occupy 151 square feet, down from 225 square feet in 2010.[8]

This may be the case for a narrow range of office jobs such as call centers and customer service. But it is unlikely to be the case for the majority of office workers. It may also be unlikely as a whole. For instance, I compared year-end office space consumption per worker for all years during the 2000s that CoStar[9] reported and found no significant difference. The mean has remained about 320 square feet per worker, or about the same as I have reported elsewhere (Nelson 2004).

For one thing, there is a difference between the actual space used by a worker—a cubicle for instance—and all other space in an office building. That space includes lobbies, conference rooms, information technology service rooms, restrooms, elevators, staircases, and so forth. Many modern office buildings include day care centers, exercise areas, and cafeterias. So, although the actual space occupied for any given worker may decline, the overall average per worker may not change much. I am thus assuming no substantial change in overall average space needs per worker between 2010 and 2030.

### Internet Substitution of Retail Space

The explosive growth in Internet retail sales would seem to portend less demand for retailing square feet in the future. Between 1998 and 1999, retail "e-commerce" increased from $5 billion to $15 billion—a threefold increase,[10] and in 2000 nearly doubled again, to $29 billion.[11] However, e-commerce sales accounted for less than 1 percent of all retail sales in 2000. Between 2002 and 2012, e-commerce retail sales increased more than 10 percent per year compounded, yet by 2012 such sales still accounted for less than 5 percent of all sales.[12] At this pace, e-commerce will account for less than 13 percent of all retail sales by 2030, though I concede it could be as high as 20 percent by 2020.[13]

There are two important points about the role of e-commerce in projecting nonresidential space needs. First, e-commerce depends on large-scale warehousing operations, so goods are shipped from the manufacturer to the warehouse and then to the consumer. Second, just because e-commerce reduces in-store retail sales does not mean the demand for retail space will fall, at least by much. For one thing, e-commerce is often merely a substitute for mail-order sales. For another, many firms are using their stores as places for e-commerce shoppers to pick up or return goods.[14] Moreover, in a growing number of cases, e-commerce firms are creating their own stores to provide direct customer service and sell more goods. Apple, Inc.'s stores are a leading example, but there are a growing number of others.[15]

There are two additional reasons why I do not expect much if any reduction in retail space demand in the United States, though retailing functions themselves will certainly change. Some retail activities defy e-commerce, especially restaurants, coffee shops, bars, and beauty salons. Moreover, the best way to comparison shop is by seeing, touching, and in some cases, trying on the goods. The Internet is a poor substitute for accurately gauging color, texture, feel, and smell. Humans are, after all, tactile, olfactory, and social creatures—hands-on retail activities are as old as human civilization.

To estimate space needs per worker, I used the total square feet of space for each category of activities reported by the US Department of Energy's Commercial Buildings Energy Consumption Survey[16] and the Manufacturing Energy Consumption Survey,[17] and divided that space by workers in each activity group for the respective years. The result is the average square feet per worker for all workers in the industrial and nonindustrial categories reported in table 4.2.

I apply those figures to Woods & Poole's estimates of employees in each economic sector and aggregate them into a total amount of space estimated to be supported by the economy.

However, there is another consideration: nonresidential space is not as durable as residential units. The typical residential unit can last nearly two centuries and perhaps longer. In contrast, the typical nonresidential space lasts on average around forty to forty-five years, as illustrated in figure 4.1. Over time, nonresidential space will need to be recycled through demolition, rebuilding, or repurposing through renovations that renew the structure for new kinds of uses.

The speed with which nonresidential structures are recycled depends on two major factors: the rate of depreciation of the building and the rate of appreciation of the land on which it sits. Buildings depreciate at widely varying rates. Depreciation for most kinds of properties ranges from about thirty years to about sixty years. But this assumes the structure is used until its intended purpose has run its course. In dynamic metropolitan areas, few nonresidential structures are used for their intended purpose through the expected useful life of

*Table 4.2* Estimated square feet of space consumed per industrial worker and nonindustrial worker.

| Land use | Square feet per worker[a] |
|---|---|
| *Industrial* | |
| Utilities | 300 |
| Manufacturing | 900 |
| Transportation & warehousing | 1,800 |
| Wholesale trade | 1,300 |
| | |
| *Nonindustrial* | |
| Office | 300 |
| Education and the arts | 750 |
| Lodging and food service | 720 |
| Retail trade | 605 |
| Health care | 500 |

*Sources:* Nonindustrial space estimated from Commercial Buildings Energy Consumption Survey (CBECS), Energy Information Administration, 2005, www.eia.gov/emeu/cbecs/cbecs2003 /detailed_tables_2003/detailed_tables_2003.html. Industrial space estimated from CBECS and Manufacturing Energy Consumption Survey, Energy Information Administration, 2009, www.eia.gov/emeu/mecs/mecs2006/2006tables.html.
[a] Space includes all occupied areas such as work spaces, lobbies, conference rooms, assembly areas, hallways, elevator shafts, etc.; collateral service functions such as cafeterias, theaters, exercise and day care; and vacant space. Figures are rounded.

the building. This is because as the structure value depreciates, land value usually appreciates, and at some point the land is worth more than the structure. The owner of the structure may see a better return on investment by recycling the land use.

Consider how the recycling decision is made. Assume the structure has a depreciable life of fifty years, which is a common period for many nonresidential structures. Suppose that when the structure is built, about 80 percent of the total property value is in the structure itself and 20 percent is in the land. Suppose also that the average annual appreciation of land (after inflation) is 1 percent. A fifty-year structure depreciating at 2 percent annually with land appreciating at 1 per-

*Figure 4.1* National average lifespan of major building classes before recycling.

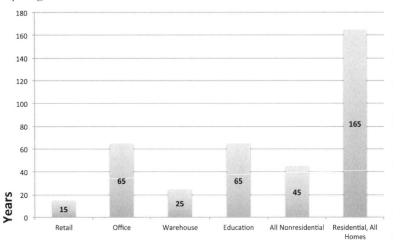

*Source*: Nonresidential figures based on the Commercial Buildings Energy Consumption Survey for 1992 and 2003, US Department of Energy, www.eia.gov/emeu/cbecs/cbecs2003/detailed _tables_2003/detailed_tables_2003.html. Figure by J. P. Goates

cent annually (compounded) will be worth less than the land in about the thirty-third year. This is illustrated in figure 4.2. It is at about the twenty-fifth year, if not before, that the property owner begins to consider demolishing and building a new structure, or renovating the existing structure (perhaps adding to it) to serve a higher and better use. I call this "recycling." However, the actual moment of recycling is often delayed until market forces justify the cost of demolition and reinvestment. The building may be used for low-rent activities in the meantime. Assuming all the nonresidential stock is built for a fifty-year useful life, the equivalent of the entire nonresidential stock in the United States recycles about every forty years.[18]

For this analysis, we will assume that the average life of all nonresidential structures will be fifty years. Certainly, some structures such as cheaply built big-box stores may become ripe for recycling after just fifteen years or so, although class A, high-rise office buildings may last a century or longer. The average may underestimate the pace at which

*Figure 4.2* Recycling ripeness of fifty-year depreciation structures. A fifty-year building depreciating at 2 percent annually on land whose value appreciates at 1 percent annually (after inflation) will be worth less than the land in the thirty-third year. This is the point after which the structure is likely to be recycled.

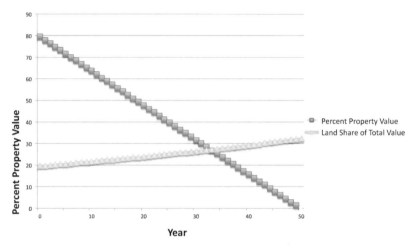

Figure by J. P. Goates

nonresidential structures will become ripe for recycling considering land value appreciation. In addition, I start the depreciation clock in 2010; that is, I estimate ripeness for recycling assuming all existing structures were built in 2010. This will also underestimate the total supply of nonresidential structures that may be replaced or repurposed by 2030. I make one more adjustment. Based on the discussion for figure 4.2, I estimate the average annual rate of growth for each geographic unit of analysis between 2010 and 2030, and use this to accelerate the conversion rate. Suppose the projected population growth in a given metropolitan area over twenty years is 20 percent. Then suppose the depreciation rate for the class of structures is fifty years. I adjust the effective life from fifty years to forty years ($50 \times (1-0.20) = 40$). Thus, the rate of population growth will accelerate the pace of structure replacement/repurposing over time.

Table 4.3 reports the net change to the inventory for all nonresidential land uses for the nation and census regions and divisions.

For a breakdown by state or by land use types, see www.ReshapeMetro America.org.

We see that the nation will need to increase its inventory of non-residential space by almost twenty-four billion square feet between 2010 and 2030, or about 28 percent more square feet than in 2010. But more than twice that, about fifty-three billion square feet, will be

Table 4.3 Nonresidential space supported, net additions to inventory, and replaced/repurposed space for the nation and census regions and divisions (figures in millions.)

| Geographic area | Total space supported, 2010 | Total space supported, 2030 | Net change in total space supported (2010–2030) | Total space replaced (2010–2030) | Total space built (2010–2030) | Total space built 2010–2030 as share of total space in 2010 (%) |
|---|---|---|---|---|---|---|
| United States | 83,349 | 106,908 | 23,558 | 52,924 | 76,482 | 92 |
| *Census regions* | | | | | | |
| Northeast | 15,258 | 18,544 | 3,287 | 8,567 | 11,854 | 78 |
| Midwest | 18,816 | 22,676 | 3,860 | 10,975 | 14,834 | 79 |
| South | 30,800 | 41,661 | 10,860 | 21,170 | 32,031 | 104 |
| West | 18,475 | 24,027 | 5,552 | 12,212 | 17,763 | 96 |
| *Census divisions* | | | | | | |
| New England | 5,994 | 7,462 | 1,468 | 3,273 | 4,741 | 79 |
| Mid Atlantic | 9,264 | 11,082 | 1,818 | 5,347 | 7,166 | 77 |
| East North Central | 11,850 | 13,790 | 1,940 | 6,841 | 8,781 | 74 |
| West North Central | 6,966 | 8,886 | 1,920 | 4,220 | 6,140 | 88 |
| South Atlantic | 14,532 | 19,636 | 5,103 | 10,379 | 15,482 | 107 |
| East South Central | 6,038 | 8,189 | 2,151 | 3,846 | 5,997 | 99 |
| West South Central | 10,230 | 13,836 | 3,606 | 7,285 | 10,890 | 106 |
| Mountain | 7,280 | 9,637 | 2,357 | 4,841 | 7,198 | 99 |
| Pacific | 11,195 | 14,389 | 3,194 | 7,607 | 10,801 | 96 |

Note: Percentages may not sum due to rounding.
[a] Figures in millions of square feet. For a state-by-state breakdown, see www.ReshapeMetroAmerica.org.

recycled. For the nation as a whole, I estimate that about seventy-six billion square feet of nonresidential space will be built or rebuilt between 2010 and 2030. This is about 92 percent of the nonresidential space that existed in 2010.

In my view, it is the sheer volume of nonresidential space to be recycled and the land it sits on that can substantially reshape metropolitan America. I will discuss how in the next chapter relating to the Reshape America Index.

# 5

# THE RESHAPE AMERICA INDEX

In this book I show that by 2030, one-quarter to one-third of America's 143 million households will want the very kinds of options provided in mixed-use, amenity-rich, transit-accessible options that commercial corridors and nodes can provide. Because about ten million households have those options now, the nation will need to increase its supply by at least twenty-five million to meet demand in 2030. In effect, if all new homes built in America between 2010 and 2030 were built in those locations, demand for this option would still not be met.

Another roughly eleven million homes will need to be replaced between 2010 and 2030, and most of them will be replaced in growing metropolitan areas (see chapter 3). How many homes will replace each home demolished? There are no statistics for this. A single home on a lot of more than one acre can be replaced by a small subdivision. Or it could simply be replaced by a larger home. In higher density areas, a single home on one acre may be replaced with ten or more housing units on the same lot. In some cases, whole neighborhoods will be bought out by public, private, or public-private ventures, removing a few to a few dozen homes and replacing them with multiple more (see Malloy 2008). At a minimum, I assume that each home demolished will be replaced with an average of four. The eleven million homes to be demolished will thus make way for forty-four million new homes and a net gain of thirty-three million homes.

In chapter 4, I showed that about half of all nonresidential structures existing in 2010 will become ripe for redevelopment by 2030.

Most of these are one-floor structures, which account for 40 percent of the nonresidential space. Together with two-floor structures, these low-rise structures account for about two-thirds of the nonresidential, nonindustrial space in the United States.[i] These structures have very low floor-area ratios (FAR).

Where will the demand for new development go? I assume that all new development between 2010 and 2030 can occur as infill and redevelopment—mostly the redevelopment of parking lots and the obsolete, low-rise structures sitting on them, along commercial corridors and at activity centers (see chapter 6).

Although parking lots and deteriorating low-rise structures may sound more like liabilities than assets, I believe they provide America with an unprecedented opportunity to meet emerging market needs by simply reshaping that which is already built.

In particular, many of these spaces have attributes making them ideal for redevelopment:

- They are already flat and reasonably well drained, so this part of the development process is largely finished.
- Almost all of these sites sit along major highways with four or more lanes, often with wide rights-of-way for easements. Because they are along multilane corridors that connect urban and suburban nodes, these sites are transit-ready.
- Large-scale utilities run along those major highways and are easily accessed for upgrading, if needed. As they age, these utilities will need to be replaced. The conundrum facing local governments is whether to (1) approve new greenfield development where initial utility capital costs are low, or (2) brace for the upgrades of major utility infrastructure along built-out corridors that would have to be done anyway and at lower long-term cost per unit of service delivery. Prudent fiscal management would seem to favor the latter investment option.
- Prior rezoning decisions often removing them from residential categories, combined with development over the years, has already committed these sites to other than low-density residential development.

- These sites have motivated owners interested in maximizing their return. This is important because impediments to redevelopment include the inability to assemble multiple, small ownerships (with clear title) and gain the confidence of owners that it is in their best interest to redevelop. This is not the case with most large commercially developed sites.
- As these sites age—and we know from chapter 4 that most of them age rapidly—the deterioration of structures compromises the value of nearby residential property.
- Those residential neighbors may be motivated to simultaneously deflect development pressure away from their neighborhoods to these aging commercial sites, especially if they have a constructive say in how they are redeveloped. In other words, potential NIMBYs (not in my backyard) may become YIMBYs (yes in my backyard).

The vast supply of parking lots and rapidly depreciating nonresidential structures presents America with an unusual opportunity to reshape its built environment. To demonstrate this, I developed the Reshape America Index (RAI), which I apply to all the geographic units I report in this book. The RAI is simply a measure of how much the average baseline FAR existing in 2010 needs to be increased to accommodate the net new nonresidential space needed between 2010 and 2030, plus all new housing units needed. RAI is calculated using this formula:

RAI = [(new nonresidential space inventory + new residential space) /
existing nonresidential space] x 100

Given the vastness of low-density suburban development, the RAI assumes that the average land-use intensity of existing metropolitan-wide development can be doubled without triggering major design solutions for parking and access.

For residential development, I assume fifteen hundred square feet per unit on infill and redevelopment sites, which includes common areas within attached-unit structures, such as hallways, activity rooms, storage areas, stairways, and so forth. With twenty-six million housing units added to the inventory between 2010 and 2030, this comes to about thirty-nine billion square feet. About twenty-four billion square feet will be added to the inventory of nonresidential space (see chapter 4). Combined, I estimate a net gain of about sixty-two billion square feet of net new residential and nonresidential space over the period 2010 to 2030. We know from table 4.3 that the United States currently supports eighty-three billion square feet of nonresidential space. The RAI score for the nation is thus:

RAI = [(62 billion square feet net new nonresidential & residential space) / (83 billion square feet supported nonresidential space)] x 100 = 74.7

Table 5.1 gives the RAI and related figures for the nation and census regions and divisions. The higher the RAI score, the more likely infill and redevelopment will not accommodate all development needs between 2010 and 2030. The South Atlantic census division, for instance, has an RAI score of 109 which means that all but 9 percent of net new developed space between 2010 and 2030 can be accommodated through infill and redevelopment; the remaining share may need some greenfield development. Yet, because my land-use intensity (FAR) assumption is based on existing levels, which are usually quite low (less than 0.20 in most metropolitan areas), RAI scores of more than 100 do not necessarily require greenfield development. Conversely, the lower the score, the more likely all development can be accommodated as infill and redevelopment. This is the case for most of the nation.

There are a number of qualifications and cautionary observations that can reduce redevelopment opportunities. For instance, tearing down the old to replace it with something more contemporary or at higher density is not necessarily good in all cases. Preservation of neighborhoods to advance community character, create stability in the market, and even to elevate long-term property values are among many reasons to preserve older structures. Nonetheless, many older structures sit on larger tracts of land that can be redeveloped, and older structures can be repurposed (from warehousing to office or residential) while retaining their historical and architectural character.[2] My

Table 5.1 Reshape America Index for the nation, and census regions and divisions (figures in millions of square feet)

| Geographic area | Net new residential space @ 1,500 sq.ft. per unit | Net change in nonresidential space, 2010–2030[a] | Total net change to built stock | Nonresidential space supported, 2010 | Reshape America Index | Amount of net new space in non-infill or redevelopment locations | Percent of net new space in non-infill or redevelopment locations |
|---|---|---|---|---|---|---|---|
| United States | 38,705 | 23,558 | 62,263 | 83,349 | 74.7 | 0 | 0.0% |
| *Census regions* | | | | | | | |
| Northeast | 3,195 | 3,287 | 6,481 | 15,258 | 42.5 | 0 | 0.0% |
| Midwest | 4,113 | 3,860 | 7,973 | 18,816 | 42.4 | 0 | 0.0% |
| South | 20,257 | 10,860 | 31,118 | 30,800 | 101.0 | 317 | 1.0% |
| West | 11,140 | 5,552 | 16,692 | 18,475 | 90.3 | 0 | 0.0% |
| *Census divisions* | | | | | | | |
| New England | 1,130 | 1,468 | 2,598 | 5,994 | 43.4 | 0 | 0.0% |
| Mid Atlantic | 2,064 | 1,818 | 3,883 | 9,264 | 41.9 | 0 | 0.0% |
| East North Central | 2,171 | 1,940 | 4,110 | 11,850 | 34.7 | 0 | 0.0% |
| West North Central | 1,942 | 1,920 | 3,862 | 6,966 | 55.4 | 0 | 0.0% |
| South Atlantic | 10,736 | 5,103 | 15,839 | 14,532 | 109.0 | 1,307 | 8.3% |
| East South Central | 2,336 | 2,151 | 4,488 | 6,038 | 74.3 | 0 | 0.0% |
| West South Central | 7,185 | 3,606 | 10,791 | 10,230 | 105.5 | 560 | 5.2% |
| Mountain | 4,572 | 2,357 | 6,929 | 7,280 | 95.2 | 0 | 0.0% |
| Pacific | 6,568 | 3,194 | 9,763 | 11,195 | 87.2 | 0 | 0.0% |

*Note:* Percentages may not sum due to rounding. For a state-by-state breakdown, see www.ReshapeMetroAmerica.org.

purpose here is to offer the broad perspective that most nonresidential development existing in urban and suburban areas in the United States may not be worth preserving, but instead is at the heart of reshaping metropolitan America.

Second, will low-intensity parcels be redeveloped at a density to support walkable, mixed-use, transit-oriented neighborhoods? This is uncertain. In most metropolitan areas, land values increase over time at least in proportion to population growth, and the higher the land value the more intensively land needs to be used to justify the cost of acquiring the property and redeveloping it. Indeed, a major road block to timely redevelopment is uncertainty by property owners about when to redevelop; they usually err on the side of caution so that redevelopment is deferred perhaps longer than may be most efficient. Public officials and planners need to be proactive in identifying those parcels that may become ripe for redevelopment within various time frames—such as between 2010 and 2030, and beyond—and then facilitate redevelopment.

Unfortunately, there is a third reason that property is probably not efficiently redeveloped: local land use policies. For instance, Arora (2007) inventoried parking requirements of selected cities in the New York metropolitan area and found minimum parking requirements ranged from about ten stalls per one thousand square feet of gross leasable area for restaurants, about seven stalls per one thousand square feet for medical offices, and about five stalls per one thousand square feet for offices and retail. Parking requirements greater than about four stalls per one thousand square feet for nonresidential land uses result in about three-quarters of the land area devoted to parking, access, and associated storm water management. A study by the Transportation Research Board concluded that for business parks, a parking ratio of 2.0 stalls per one thousand square feet of building space is sufficient to take care of the overall needs (Kuzmyak et al. 2003).

The bottom line is that the place where most of this redevelopment can occur will be in suburbia. It is where most Americans live and where most jobs are found (Lang 2003). Suburbia consists mostly of low-rise structures along commercial corridors with occasional activity nodes, also at low-intensity use. "Retrofitting suburbia"

(Dunham-Jones and Williamson 2008) can turn transit-ready corridors into transit corridors, and can transform dowdy suburban centers into vibrant, mixed-use ones. Virtually all of America's development needs between 2010 and 2030, and beyond, can be accommodated by retrofitting suburbs, and this can be done without invading established residential neighborhoods.

The RAI is pioneering, so I hope it gives a perspective to public officials and real estate development interests about the potential for new growth to be accommodated on existing parking lots.

# 6

# THE BENEFITS OF RESHAPING METROPOLITAN AMERICA

What if Americans got what they wanted? To be more specific, what if the one-quarter to one-third of Americans who want to be able to walk or bike to work and for errands lived in communities that had this option? What if the 25–33 percent of Americans who want the option to walk or bike to transit (other than conventional bus) lived in places where they could? What if the half of Americans who prefer to live in a smart growth community instead of a sprawling one actually did? To achieve this by 2030, virtually all new development between 2010 and 2030 would need to be in communities providing these options. If this were to happen, what would be the benefits?

For this "thought" exercise, I assume that all new development between 2010 and 2030 occurs as infill and redevelopment—mostly the redevelopment of parking lots and the obsolete, low-rise structures sitting on them along commercial corridors and at activity centers (see chapter 5). I consider environmental, economic, and social benefits of this reshaping of America compared to business as usual. For perspective, in table 6.1, I compare reshaping America to sprawl in terms of density, growth patterns, and other factors (see Litman 2006).

*Table 6.1* Reshaping America versus business-as-usual.

| Feature | Reshaping America | Business as usual |
| --- | --- | --- |
| Density | Higher density, clustered activities | Lower density, dispersed activities |
| Growth patterns | Infill (brownfield) and redevelopment | Urban periphery (greenfield) development |
| Land use mix | Mixed land use | Homogeneous (single-use, segregated) land uses |
| Scale | Human scale; smaller buildings, blocks, and roads; designed for pedestrians | Large scale; larger blocks, wider roads; less detail because people experience landscape at a distance and as motorists |
| Services (shops, schools, parks) | Local, distributed, smaller; accommodate walking access | Regional, consolidated, larger; require automobile access |
| Transport | Multimodal transport and land use patterns that support walking, biking, and transit | Automobile-oriented transport and land use patterns; poorly suited for walking, biking, and transit |
| Connectivity | Highly connected roads, sidewalks, and paths | Hierarchical road network with numerous dead-end streets, and unconnected paths and sidewalks |
| Street design | Streets designed to accommodate a variety of activities; traffic calming | Streets designed to maximize motor vehicle traffic volume and speed |
| Planning process | Planned and coordinated between jurisdictions and stakeholders | Unplanned, with little coordination between jurisdictions and stakeholders |
| Public realm | Emphasis on the public realm (streets, sidewalks, and parks) | Emphasis on the private realm (yards, shopping malls, gated communities) |

*Source*: Adapted from Litman (2006) with permission.

## THE MARKET PREFERENCE SCENARIO

The over-arching theme is that it is the market that wants certain changes to the built landscape. If we heed market preferences, we will reshape America in ways that confer important environmental, economic and social benefits. However, many of our institutions are barriers to achieving market-driven preferences. How we should change them is the subject of the last chapter.

I have shown that in most of the nation all new residential units and jobs can go into infill and redevelopment places that are already developed, especially commercial corridors and urban and suburban activity centers. Let us assume that it does.

Before proceeding, I need to make a qualification. My assessment of the "market" is based on stated preferences surveys which can differ from "revealed" preferences. A person might say he or she want a home near transit but given a choice, may choose a home in the suburbs nowhere near transit. Of course, one problem is that the supply of options may be too thin or non-existent, so there may actually be little choice but to move to the suburbs. Moreover, many choices are skewed by public policies that distort options. (I will discuss these problems and their solutions in the next chapter.)

Nonetheless, there is ample "revealed" preference evidence to support stated performance surveys. Here is a partial list:

- Homes in "new urbanism" communities appreciate faster and hold their value better during downtowns than homes in conventional subdivisions (Tu and Eppli 1999).[1]
- Homes in neighborhoods with higher "walk scores" sell for more than homes in neighborhoods with lower walk scores, all things considered (Cortright 2009).[2]
- Resale prices of homes in mixed-income and mixed-housing neighborhoods are higher than resale prices of homes in homogenous neighborhoods (Pollakowski et al. 2005).
- Homes are more valuable the closer they are to rail transit (Mathur and Ferrell 2009). This also applies to homes closer to bus rapid transit stations (Perk and Catalá 2009)

- Commercial property value rises the closer it is to transit stations (Cervero et al. 2004).
- Commercial property values are higher in mixed-use developments, including residential components, than in single-use developments (Minadeo 2009).

It would seem that stated preference surveys and revealed preference studies say the same thing: Americans want mixed-use neighborhoods, walkability, and proximity to workplaces, errands, and transit options. America's commercial companies also value mixed-use developments and accessibility to transit.

So, what are the environmental, economic, and social benefits to reshaping America compared to business as usual development?

## ENVIRONMENTAL BENEFITS

Environmental benefits include open space preservation with important ecosystem service benefits, reduced energy consumption, and lower carbon emissions. Let us consider each of these.

### Open Space Preservation and Ecosystem Service Benefits

Between 1987 and 2007, the United States added sixty million people—about 25 percent. During that time, its consumption of land for urban uses increased by about thirty-four million acres—about 66 percent.[3] This is more than one and one-half acres of land developed for every new household added. Assuming no change in land consumption, the trend would have another forty million acres of land developed for urban uses between 2010 and 2030—an area larger than the state of Georgia. If all new development occurred on existing developed land or as infill of vacant parcels in urbanized areas, the loss of open spaces could be substantially diminished. Although estimating the economic value of open spaces not developed is based on many factors, not the least of which are the kinds of open spaces preserved and agreement on their economic value,[4] a crude estimate is $6,000 per acre annually in the United States (see Sutton and Costanza 2002).[5]

This value is returned annually and across future generations. It is a nonmarket value in the sense that a person's willingness to pay for open space does not reflect such future, intergenerational benefits as reducing greenhouse effects, protecting the ozone layer, preventing environmental destruction, avoiding natural resource depletion, and advancing biodiversity and endangered species (Cowan 2001). These would be considered "public goods" because no one can be excluded from enjoying these benefits (by paying a fee, for instance) and everyone benefits equally (there is no congestion effect in the enjoyment of benefits), so they defy valuation in the private market.

What is the present value of this annual value? That is, if there were a market for these services from open spaces and the value was $6,000 per year per acre, what is the value today of the stream of benefits over time? This is called the intergenerational value. Mertens and Rubinchik (2006) calculated a present value based on growth in consumption per capita, which is akin to annual gross domestic product. Using this method, over one hundred years, the present value of an acre of open space not developed would be in the range of about $265,000 per acre.[6] If forty million acres of open spaces are not developed, society benefits by more than $10 trillion over the next century.

## Reduced Energy Consumption

The thesis of *Reshaping Metropolitan America* is that nearly all new development can be accommodated as infill or redevelopment mostly in suburban areas that are dominated by low-density/intensity land uses. According to the EPA if new residential development were to occur in infill locations instead of suburban fringe/exurban ones, miles traveled per vehicle and energy consumption associated with vehicular use would fall to about 60 percent of current levels (Environmental Protection Agency 2007). In addition, research of the Jonathan Rose Companies (2011) indicates that if all new residential and employment growth went into existing developed areas, vehicle miles traveled (VMT) combined with reduced building energy consumption would be reduced by a third or more compared to having that development occur in suburban fringe or exurban areas.

Wilson and Navaro (2007) found that traveling to buildings often uses as much energy as is consumed in the building. When taking this into consideration the Jonathan Rose Companies finds that compared to living in a typical single-family detached home in an auto-dependent suburb, living in an energy-efficient attached home in a suburban location can reduce total building and transportation energy consumption up to 64 percent. Living in such a home in an urban location can reduce consumption by up to 75 percent.

Consider also that about 85 percent of the energy consumed in the United States is produced from fossil fuels, with 39 percent from petroleum and equal shares from natural gas and coal (23 percent each).[7] Transportation consumes about 29 percent of all energy produced in the United States, almost all from petroleum. Industrial users consume another 21 percent; residential and commercial uses consume 10 percent. The rest, 40 percent, is consumed by energy-producing facilities (Randolph 2008). In effect, reducing the consumption of fossil fuels by end users will also reduce the use of energy for production. Adjusting for the energy used to produce energy, transportation consumes nearly half (48 percent) of all energy, industry about a third (35 percent), and commercial and residential uses about 17 percent. Indeed, transportation alone accounts for more than 70 percent of all fossil fuel consumption in the United States, and about half (49 percent) of this fossil fuel comes from other countries.[8]

Finally, just as density and urban form influence VMT and associated greenhouse gases, so they also influence building energy use. Except for very large buildings, generally the larger the structure the less energy is consumed per square foot. Data from the Commercial Buildings Energy Consumption Survey for 2003 (Energy Information Administration 2006) indicate that energy consumption per square foot falls by about 30 percent between buildings under 5,000 square feet and those of 10,000–25,000 square feet, which accounts for the largest share of all commercial buildings. Buildings over 100,000 square feet consume more energy per square foot, but this is changing as technology improves.[9] There is another relationship affecting residential buildings. Generally, the less square feet that are contained in a building the more energy for building materials and operations is consumed per person (by 2.5 times) and per square foot (by 1.5 times), (Norman et al. 2006).[10]

In chapter 2 we saw that about 39 percent of American households want the option to live in attached homes such as apartments, condominiums, and townhouses, yet fewer than 30 percent of American households live in those types of dwellings. To meet the market demand, nearly every new unit built in the United States between 2010 and 2030 would have be attached, twenty-one million units of the twenty-six million units needed. Meeting market needs can result in substantial energy consumption savings.

*Lower Carbon Emissions*

If all new development occurs on existing developed land, two things happen to the consumption of fossil fuels. First, miles traveled per vehicle may go down because the outward spread of urbanization is halted. Second, new development on existing developed parcels can reduce the distances between origin and destination. As VMT is reduced, so are the greenhouse gases that science has found to influence global climate change (see Ewing et al. 2008). How much the reduction is depends on the nature of future development patterns, the role of public transit in shifting mode choice, and how walking and biking modes are affected. Still, generally, if all new development occurs in existing developed areas as infill or redevelopment, overall residential and employment density will increase by about 20 percent. Because VMT is somewhat elastic to changing density, a 20 percent increase in density through infill and redevelopment may reduce VMT per vehicle by about 10 percent (Ewing et al. 2008). The overall effect would be less miles traveled per vehicle in 2030 than in 2010 though on the whole higher total VMT. Alternatively, if new development occurs where transit and walking/biking are significant mobility options, and in compact versus low-density patterns, total VMT in 2030 can be reduced to below 2010 levels (see Ewing 2008).

Litman (2012) observed that although individual infill and redevelopment designs may have modest impacts that each reduce VMT by just a few percentage points, together they have cumulative and synergetic impacts (see also Blais 2010; Transportation Research Board 2009; ICF Consulting 2011). Litman (2010) observes that improving walking connections between land uses, encouraging multiple mode choices, and increasing density each reduce VMT in the range of 2–4 percent. But when infill and redevelopment projects are coordinated, the cumulative and synergistic reductions range up to 50 percent or more where transit is an option, and up to 40 percent for auto-dependent projects.

## ECONOMIC BENEFITS

Several economics benefits will result from accommodating all future growth in existing developed areas, such as creating agglomeration economies, elevating the economic development returns of transportation investments, increasing property values, and creating a more resilient fiscal base.

### Creating Agglomeration Economies

Urban areas are economic development dynamos. The bigger and the more densely settled they are, the more economic wealth they produce (Glaeser 2011). If the market is allowed to integrate land uses, increase transportation options, and increase housing density and employment intensity, it will make our urban areas more economically productive. This will reduce unemployment, increase wages, and make economies more resilient to downturns.

Metropolitan areas tend to grow faster and generate more wealth when they can take advantage of *agglomeration economies*, which is shorthand for the idea—and empirically, the fact—that economic development is enhanced by a clustering of economic activity, usually through employment density. Agglomeration economies are fundamental to metropolitan growth and to resilience to economic change over time.

Generally, the more densely settled an area the more jobs per capita, the higher incomes, the lower unemployment, and the more resilient it is to economic downturns. Although less densely settled areas may grow faster, densely settled ones grow better in terms of income, wages, and job accessibility. In a pioneering study, Ciccone and Hall (1996) found that doubling employment density increases labor productivity by about 6 percent. A subsequent study by Harris and Ioannides (2002) found that a doubling of population density also increases labor productivity by about 6 percent. Bettencourt et al. (2007) found that a doubling of the population density increased economic productivity by 15 percent. This would be on top of the jobs and wages that would occur anyway. These economic development benefits accrue across most economic sectors.

Let us take the lower of these estimates. An increase of jobs (a measure of both economic and labor productivity) by 6 percent with a doubling of density is not trivial. In 2009, the average occupied single-family home sat on a lot of about 12,000 square feet.[11] If lot size were half this, or about 6,000 square feet (roughly the standard subdivision lot of the 1960s), and other land uses were adjusted accordingly, *at this higher density there would be 10 million more jobs in the United States,*[12] or more than the six million jobs lost during the Great Recession.[13] This is on top of the jobs that would exist anyway.

Higher densities also spur innovation as more opportunities for collaboration are created. Innovation is needed to sustain economic development over time. For instance, Jaffe et al. (1993) showed that ideas move more quickly when people are in higher density settings. Patents are a good indicator of innovation. After controlling for location, education, and other factors, Carlino et al. (2006) found that a doubling of residential density increases patent activity by 20 percent. Because innovation presages future economic development, this is an important benefit of agglomeration economies associated with density. Lucas and Rossi-Hansberg (2002) went further by showing that higher density increases the speed of production—another twist on the "time is money" slogan.

Moreover, higher densities improve resilience to economic downturns. A study by the Federal Reserve Board (Wheeler, 2005) showed that higher density urban areas improve job-searching options for workers as both they and their employers strive for maximum economic productivity. Lower density urban areas simply do not have the thresholds needed to stimulate job production and skill matching.

Agglomeration economies are especially important to such postindustrial economic sectors as retail and services. If density is too low, an area may not support certain kinds of retail and service activities; spending that does not occur in the area then goes to other areas, including outside the region. If it is too far or inconvenient to drive to shop, some spending goes to the Internet or some purchases are simply not made. The trouble is that many metropolitan areas have designed themselves to eliminate economic development by reducing density thresholds needed to maximize retail and service trade.

They do this through one or more beltways that disperse population and employment growth. A study by a colleague and me (Nelson and Moody 2000) found that a metropolitan area of two million residents with one beltway (such as Kansas City) loses $1.8 billion in retail and service sales annually, while those with two (such as San Antonio) lose $2.3 billion annually (in 2012 dollars). This equates to about 68,000 and 85,000 jobs, respectively.[14] Roughly speaking, of the thirty metropolitan areas with at least one beltway, the nation's employment base had about three million jobs fewer than there would be without the beltways. This is about half of the six million jobs that were lost to the Great Recession.[15]

There is another consideration: Agglomeration economies lead to higher incomes. Glaeser and Kahn (2003) reviewed the literature and undertook their own study to confirm this. They found that, "These papers all suggest that sprawl might indeed reduce agglomeration economies and deter overall productivity" (p. 40). They demonstrated, using econometric analysis, that higher metropolitan-level density results in higher per capita income. They also showed that although aggregate density at the metropolitan level matters, the degree to which jobs are centralized in the central city does not appear to be important (p. 41). This is consistent with my view that most agglomeration economy gains are made when suburban areas become more densely settled in both jobs and people. Ciccone and Hall also (1996) found a connection between county-level density and economic agglomeration leading to higher wages. In another study, Glaeser and Mare (2001) showed that higher wages are not the result of workers moving to urban areas but that urban areas make them more productive.

What would we have if all new development occurred in existing developed areas between 2010 and 2030? The change would be a roughly 20 percent increase in average density nationally. There would be about 1.2 percent or about 2.3 million more jobs[16] nationally than would occur if development occurred in greenfields, thus reducing the future unemployment rate substantially below what it would be otherwise.[17] Incomes would be higher. There would be perhaps 20 percent more innovation than if density were not increased in the aggregate. Without innovation, the United States loses competitiveness globally.

As a key ingredient to facilitating market trends toward agglomeration and the economic benefits they confer, however we will need to change our transportation investment strategies.

*Elevating Economic Returns from Transportation Investments*

The literature finds that transportation investments that lower population and employment density also reduce economic productivity over time, and transportation investments that attract growth into nodes or corridors improve economic productivity by increasing density.

It is thus important to make the transportation investments that support where the market is going rather than making investments in infrastructure that support single-family subdivisions where values are already declining. More is at stake than just meeting the demand for access to public transportation. Sustained economic development depends in large part on engaging as many people as possible in the economy. For the broad economy it is often better for someone who is unemployed to get a job than for someone who is already employed to switch jobs. Putting transit in communities with high unemployment has a disproportionately positive impact on reducing unemployment compared to putting it in communities with already low unemployment—up to 2.5 times more impact (see Ferguson and Dickens 1999). There are two main ways in which these benefits may be realized. One is by meeting the demand for public transit options, especially rail. The other is by seizing the market response to rail investments.

Ewing (2009) summarized research on the association between highway investments and agglomeration economies, and economic development. A central finding was that major highway investments have small net effects on the growth and development of metropolitan areas, instead mostly moving development around the region. Highway investment patterns tend to favor suburbs over central cities, and thereby contribute to decentralization and low-density development. Indeed, major highway investments may actually hurt regional productivity if they induce inefficient (low-density) development patterns.

Highway investments that facilitate low-density development will likely reduce jobs relative to other transportation investments, including highways that facilitate agglomeration economies along corridors connecting nodes. This is not to say that all road projects per se reduce agglomeration economies. In early stages of urbanization, roads establish initial trade among places and facilitate opportunities for firm specialization, thus leading to exports using roads. In modern times, it was only roads that created the very agglomeration economies around which urban areas were formed. Atlanta, Dallas, Denver, and Phoenix come to mind. Eventually, agglomeration economies are sustained best with multimodal options. However, even as they mature, there will often be selected highway investments that sustain or even enhance agglomeration economies. These may not be large projects, such as perimeter highways or major expressways, but arterials and collectors within the established metropolitan fabric that reduce bottlenecks, for instance.

The implication is that agglomeration economies increase with respect to labor market size. Automobile congestion can undermine agglomeration economies. The reason is that although agglomeration benefits occur because of greater accessibility—meaning more labor becomes available to employers—congestion reduces accessibility, thereby negating benefits of agglomeration. In large metropolitan areas, transit is needed to sustain agglomeration economies, especially as it connects activity nodes along corridors.[18]

There may be more opportunities for enhancing existing agglomeration economies and creating new ones through public transportation than perhaps through any other transportation investment. Unfortunately, there is not enough research into these relationships and far less such research than for highways.

Focusing development around public transportation has been a successful method for advancing environmental and quality of life goals in metropolitan areas around the country. This is commonly done through "transit-oriented developments," which have become an effective tool for achieving economic development objectives. This is not a terribly surprising result, given public transportation's historic ties to land development: most of the transit facilities developed in the early twentieth century were constructed by private entrepreneurs hoping to open new lands to commercial and residential development (Cudahy 1990). Public transportation agencies, cities, and developers are rediscovering that transit can again serve as an economic engine for local and regional economies.

Theory would also predict that increasing availability will translate into higher intensity/higher value development projects. Bartholomew and Ewing (2011) report an example of this effect. In the Pearl District, near downtown Portland, Oregon, the city constructed a new streetcar line in 1997. Before the streetcar line was built, development in the area was constructed at less than half the density (as measured by floor-area ratio) allowed by zoning. However, projects built since 1997 have been constructed at 60–90 percent of the allowable density. By 2010, more than $3.5 billion in private capital had been invested within the two blocks of the streetcar alignment, including more than ten thousand units of new housing and five million square feet of commercial space (City of Portland 2008).

Where do we go from here? If a metropolitan area already has a mature highway system, which transportation option generates the greatest returns? Recent evidence suggests that metropolitan areas gain more economic benefits from transit investments than highways (Nelson et al. 2009).

*Property Value Benefits*

A key source of wealth is the value of real property. Unfortunately, the Great Recession wiped out a good deal of real estate equity. Average home equity rose to about $200,000 in 2006, but by 2012 it had fallen to $78,000 per home,[19] a loss of nearly $10 trillion. There is some well-founded speculation that equity values may not return to 2006 levels for a generation or longer.[20]

The urban land market provides some valuable lessons in preparing for the recovery of property values in America. First, we now know that compactness of urban form and accessibility matter in the resilience of home values during economic downtowns. Second, we also know that the residential and nonresidential market rewards proximity to transit systems such as rail, streetcar, and bus rapid transit. Third, the market rewards higher density, mixed-use, and mixed-housing developments over homogeneous developments.

Bartholomew and Ewing (2011) synthesized literature showing that residential and nonresidential property values are generally higher the closer they are to fixed guideway transit systems. Another study, done by Cervero et al. (2004) reported price premiums of between 6.4 percent and 45 percent for housing located within a quarter- to a half-mile radius of rail transit stations, compared to comparable housing outside of the station areas. Premiums for commercial property values ranged from 8 percent to 12 percent along Denver's 16th Street Mall to 40 percent for the area surrounding Dallas's Mockingbird light-rail station. My own work shows that heavy-rail stations in residential areas confer a price premium on residential properties generally (Nelson and McClesky 1990) and low-income properties especially (Nelson 1992). Commercial property values also benefit by proximity to heavy-rail stations (Nelson 1999). Positive effects on both kinds of property are found with respect to light-rail, (see Mathur and Ferrell 2009) and residential values are higher with respect to bus rapid transit stations (Perk and Catalá 2009).

Both residential (Tombari 2005) and nonresidential (Minadeo 2009) property values increase when situated within higher density mixed-use, mixed-residential developments. Key ingredients for maximizing the value premium include (1) convenience of live-work-play options in a single location, such as is offered by a mixed-use development, (2) creating a small-town "Main Street" setting despite being in the middle of an urbanized area, (3) reducing traffic congestion within the development along with providing multiple mobility options, and (4) achieving the highest land use density possible (Rabianski and Clements 2007).

In theory, if a person can save money on transportation costs, those savings can be used to support owning a home. Nationally, the typical American household apportions about 49 percent of their expenditures to housing (33 percent) and transportation (16 percent).[21] But transportation costs in sprawling areas can be double or more the national average, and consume a very high share of lower- and middle-income households' earnings.[22] When a low-density suburban household loses one or two wage earners, it becomes vulnerable to foreclosure for two principal reasons. First, low-density suburban areas are not as resilient as higher density ones, so job options are constrained. This is because lower density areas do not have the densities needed to meet the threshold requirements of many kinds of retail and service companies. Second, finding a job may require commuting to a lower paying job. In either case, low-density locations are dependent on the car for accessing important destinations.

In contrast, higher density areas have the advantage of agglomeration economies that generate more jobs because of their higher density, and they offer greater accessibility to destinations. One measure of this property value benefit is the ability to walk to places. Thus, areas with higher "walk scores" should have lower rates of foreclosure[23] than areas with lower walk scores.

In a test of this, I found that a 10 percent increase in the walk score reduces the foreclosure rate by about 5.2 percent.[24]

### Creating a More Resilient Fiscal Base

There are three fiscal benefits that accrue from accommodating all future development through infill and redevelopment. First, fiscal costs are reduced because, on average, facilities are made more efficient. Second, these savings provide funds for the private sector to make investments and hire people. Third, taken together, increasing density through infill and redevelopment will reduce fiscal costs and lead to higher wages and improved economic resilience.

Theoretically, the costs of many facilities and services increase per person as density declines (Carruthers and Ulfarsson 2003). The trouble is that for the most part our local public facility and service financing schemes reward lower density development and punish higher density development. The result is that markets are distorted, leading to more high-cost development and less low-cost development.

The 2002 study by Robert Burchell, *The Costs of Sprawl—2000,* combined with his earlier *The Costs of Sprawl—Revisited* (Burchell et al. 1998), represent some of the most comprehensive research on the subject. The earlier work reviewed and synthesized the literature; the later study used that material to project the infrastructure cost implications of national "uncontrolled" and controlled growth scenarios over a twenty-five–year planning horizon. The controlled scenario had only about 10 percent of the new growth as infill and redevelopment occurring in existing developed areas. Residential development would be built at 20 percent higher density and nonresidential development would be at 10 percent higher floor-area ratio. These conservative assumptions show that the controlled growth scenario would cost about $160 billion less (in 2012 dollars) for basic infrastructure (water, sewer, and roads) than the uncontrolled scenario, a savings of about 11 percent. Using Burchell's schema, if all new development occurred in existing developed areas, the cost savings would be $700 billion or more, or just about the cost of the Troubled Asset Relief Program used to bail out financial institutions when the housing bubble of the late 2000s burst.[25]

## SOCIAL BENEFITS

Does more compact development benefit low- and moderate-income households more than sprawling development? On the whole, this seems to be the case. There are gains in affordable housing, transportation equity, and public health.

### Affordable Housing

America is schizophrenic when it comes to choosing between producing affordable housing and housing that creates equity. On the one hand, we want to be able to buy homes. Flooding the market with homes is one solution; indeed, the housing bubble of the 2000s led to the oversupply of millions of homes, thereby driving prices down. By the mid-2000s, America's housing affordability concerns were considerably less than they were a decade earlier, but not in a way that is desired.

What I advocate are regional approaches to stemming sprawl by accommodating market demands in existing urbanized—mostly suburban—areas. This would be accomplished, in part, by properly pricing infrastructure so that high-cost areas are not subsidized by low-cost areas (see Blais 2010). It would also include commitment to facilitating infill and redevelopment along transit and transit-ready corridors and nodes—meeting the needs of the third of Americans who want transit options in mixed-use settings.

Region-wide urban containment strategies can help accomplish this in ways that can actually increase the supply of affordable housing, which is another benefit of reshaping metropolitan America. Here is why.

My colleagues and I (Nelson et al. 2007) evaluated regional and subregional "urban containment" plans to assess their effects on the supply of affordable rental housing. We found that metropolitan-wide urban containment programs are associated with increased preservation of the existing affordable housing stock, while urban containment programs adopted at the submetropolitan level have no significant impacts on affordable housing supply.

Our work also found that urban containment policies are usually (though not always) accompanied by proactive affordable housing policies. We found that not all containment regimes support the preservation of the existing affordable rental housing stock. Only when an urban containment program is adopted and implemented region-wide is the impact on affordable rental housing statistically significant. This likely results from the increased coordination of affordable housing planning found within metropolitan-wide containment programs. Submetropolitan containment programs, such as those in Boulder, Colorado, and Montgomery County, Maryland, have affordable housing programs that have little impact on the regional affordable housing supply.

To some, urban containment is viewed simply as a supply-restricting mechanism, and certainly in some places this is accurate (see Nelson and Dawkins 2004). Our research suggests that although urban containment may raise housing prices because of amenity and efficiency effects, it also facilitates the preservation of the affordable rental housing stock when implemented regionally.

*Transportation Equity*

Transportation is the second largest expenditure category for American families. In 2007 US households spent on average 18 percent of their annual income on transportation.[26] Only shelter, at 33 percent, exceeds transportation. Transportation has not always consumed such a high percentage of the family budget. But as public investments in transportation began to emphasize roads and highways over public transportation, private spending on transportation increased dramatically. The resulting lack of public transportation options has shifted household spending more toward private transportation. The large initial down payment cost associated with an automobile purchase, combined with the added financing and maintenance costs, have increased the relative transportation cost burden for low-income families who rely on auto-based transportation. Families living in sprawling metropolitan areas, with little public transportation and destinations so spread out as to be unreachable by foot or bicycle, must spend even more on transportation, in some cases more than they do on rent or mortgage.

Public transportation access is a significant factor in determining average rates of labor participation in local economies (Sanchez 1999). Perhaps one reason is purely the cost of transportation, wherein households earning between twenty thousand and thirty-five thousand dollars paid two-thirds more for transportation in the suburbs where transit is not available than in the central city where transit is available (Litman 2006). Unfortunately, most jobs are found in dispersed suburban locations without reasonable, if any, public transportation access.

As families are forced to spend thousands of dollars annually on owning and operating cars and trucks (which are rapidly depreciating assets), they have less money to invest in home ownership, hindering wealth creation and the ability to enjoy other benefits of home ownership. The poorest Americans are especially hard hit, spending nearly 40 percent of their take-home pay on transportation costs, an expense that may require those families to dip into savings, borrow from relatives, and look for nontraditional sources of income to make ends meet.

We know that more compact metropolitan areas are more racially integrated than sprawling ones (Nelson et al. 2004, 2005). They also provide more mobility options and improved jobs–housing balance (Nelson and Dawkins 2004). As such, more compact metropolitan areas improve transportation equity over sprawling alternatives.

*Public Health*

By shifting all new development to existing developed areas, public health will also be improved. This happens as greenhouse gases are reduced because VMT is reduced. More compact areas also create more walking and biking options. Ewing et al. (2003) found that more compact areas are associated with a lower body mass index per capita that translates into higher longevity. Frumkin et al. (2004) showed that more sprawling urban forms lead to higher incidences of adverse public health outcomes than compact ones. Glaeser (2011) observed that higher density cities have lower mortality rates at all age groups than sprawling urban forms. According to Ewing et al. (2008), the bottom line is that having all new growth co-locate where development already exists will improve public health.

In their pioneering 2003 work, McCann and Ewing measured the degree of sprawl with a county "sprawl index" based on census and other federal data to quantify development patterns in 448 metropolitan counties across the United States. The greater the sprawl, the lower was a county's numerical value on the index. A key feature of sprawling counties is that homes are far from destinations and often the only way to access destinations is via the automobile. People living in sprawling areas are less likely to have opportunities to walk, bike, or take transit than people living in more compact areas. The research by McCann and Ewing established a direct association between sprawling versus compact urban forms and the health of the people who live there.

In particular, they found at the extreme that people living in the most sprawling county are likely to weigh six pounds more than people in the most compact county. They also found a direct relationship between sprawl and chronic disease. The Ewing et al. (2003) study also showed that sprawling metropolitan areas led residents to walk less, weigh more, and have higher prevalence of health problems linked to physical inactivity than those living in more compact places.

A related study headed by Ewing et al. (2002) used sprawl indices to make two important findings related to public health. First, areas with the highest residential densities had twenty fewer fatalities per 100,000 people than the lower density areas; and regions with the strongest centers had twelve fewer fatalities per 100,000 people than regions with the weakest centers. Second, areas with the highest urban residential density had fifty-one parts per billion lower ozone levels than the lowest urban density areas. They note that elevated levels of ozone are dangerous for children, the elderly, and asthma sufferers, among other vulnerable populations.

## SUMMARY

In the first two chapters, I documented growing market and housing preference trends for more compact development patterns. In chapter 3, I showed that emerging housing demands associated with demographic changes clearly favor more compact communities than in the past. In chapters 4 and 5, I showed that nearly all new development needs can be met through the infill and redevelopment of mostly low-density suburbanized areas, with the resulting landscape still being decidedly low density. In this chapter, I demonstrated that the weight of evidence indicates that more compact areas generate more environmental, economic, property value and social benefits than sprawling areas. In the next and final chapter I will pose a plan for reshaping metropolitan America to 2030 that aims to meet emerging market demands so these benefits can be realized.

# 7

# AGENDA TO RESHAPE
# METROPOLITAN AMERICA

America's population is getting older and more diverse, and these changes will influence housing needs. The Baby Boom generation shocked the housing system between about 1980 and 2005 by needing more new housing units than any previous generation. Because of their income and growing space needs, and the availability of cheap housing in the suburbs, their needs could be met easily through the construction of single-family homes on large lots. They accounted for three-quarters of the demand for new housing during this period, causing suburbs to expand as never before, but this trend has run its course. Because of demographic changes, the new demand for this kind of housing may only be a small fraction of the total demand to 2030.

Moreover, about a third or more of American households want different things out of their neighborhood than in the past such as mixed uses, more housing choices, improved accessibility, and more mobility options, but maybe only a tenth of American households have these options now. Even if all new development to 2030 provided these features, demand would still exceed supply. With a few isolated exceptions, continuing to build on larger lots will not meet future demand and will merely exacerbate the current excess supply. The effect could be continued erosion of housing values in overbuilt markets. Exceptions may be for larger lots as part of an overall mix in master-planned communities, and for lots where the buildable area is small but where the final lot size is increased by open spaces, easements, and other factors that contribute to sustainability.

Against this backdrop is my finding that all new residential and nonresidential development between 2010 and 2030 can probably be absorbed along existing and planned transit corridors and nodes (such as transit-oriented developments (TODs)) with only modest increases in current land use intensity. This would not be forcing on the market something it does not want; preference surveys and economic analysis indicate this is exactly where the unmet need for new residential development is.

For example, The Urban Land Institute (2010a) offered two areas of broad guidance in reshaping America's metropolitan areas:

**Compact Land Use Outcomes** Planners, builders, and investors can tap into this demand by adopting multifaceted, town-centric land use patterns, which provide greater housing and transportation choices for residents and reduce the number of vehicle miles traveled. Pedestrian-friendly neighborhoods around commercial centers (stores, restaurants, offices) with mid- and high-rise residences make public transit more feasible and lower the household cost burdens for transportation. In these places, people can meet daily needs more economically, driving less and walking or riding bikes more. Less driving helps relieve congestion and improve travel times, boosting overall system productivity and mobility. Lower electric bills in smaller homes provide an added benefit, and reduced power usage and fewer vehicle miles traveled decrease pollution and carbon emissions (Urban Land Institute 2010a, 64–65).

**Revitalizing Suburbs** A generation ago, cities struggled to implement inner-city urban renewal strategies. Now, the urban redevelopment challenge shifts to the suburbs, where an underutilized parking lot is a terrible thing to waste. Planners are refashioning abandoned shopping malls and reimagining failed retail strips, reviving subdivisions savaged in the foreclosure wave, and rethinking already entitled greenfield housing plans. In the future, depleted tax bases and declining support from federal and state coffers force more counties and towns to consolidate resources and consider regional solutions instead of cannibalistically competing for projects and new businesses. Although plenty of bulldozing is in order, revamping and retooling existing buildings and spaces takes precedence over building new ones. As roads and sewage treatment plants reach the end of their life cycles, it's time to consider implementing smarter, more integrated solutions (Urban Land Institute 2010a, 65).

However, there is a contrary view. In its 2012 edition of *The State of the Nation's Housing*, staff of the Joint Center for Housing Studies at Harvard University observed:

> The most recent Census Bureau county population estimates indicate that growth of exurban areas largely stalled by 2011 in response to the collapse of the homebuilding industry. But given that much of the undeveloped land in metropolitan areas is located in these outlying communities, there is every reason to believe that the exurbs will once again capture a disproportionate share of growth once residential construction activity revives. (Harvard Joint Center for Housing Studies 2012, 14)

A key reason for this view is offered by the Joint Center's director of research, Chris Herbert:

> How much new housing will we need when household growth gets back to normal and vacancies start to clear? About 1.6 million units a year. ... That's a lot of housing to squeeze into the existing urban and suburban infrastructure.[1]

Thus, although the demand may exist to revitalize suburbs and achieve more compact development patterns, the inertia of decades of planning and zoning designed to meet the needs of prior generations may be too much to overcome to meet the needs of future generations. The result may be continued sprawl by default.

Where do we go from here? The literature on how to reshape America is extensive. Before advancing my agenda, it is important to review what the literature says.

## THE NEW COMMUNITY PLANNING PARADIGM

Planning and community design is an ever-changing field, responding to the changing needs and preferences of the population and of employers. What was once highly valued, such as large detached homes
on large lots tens of miles from centers, is now so out of fashion that
these units may become the nation's next supply of affordable and even
multifamily housing. Segregation of land uses, once the mainstay of
zoning practices, has given way to mixed-use development as the preferred scenario in every regional long-range planning exercise conducted over the past few decades (see Bartholomew et al. 2011). Where
automobiles were the mode of choice, people now want multiple
mode choices and are willing to pay for them. These and other market
shifts are changing the face of community planning and design. Here,
I review five themes that have emerged from the literature responding
to these shifts: guiding principles to achieve sustainable communities;
the need for healthier community design; how reshaping suburbs will
meet new market challenges; the role of transit, especially TODs, in
meeting the demands of the next generation and beyond; and reforming land use regulatory system.

### Achieving Sustainable Communities

The United Nations (2009), in *Planning Sustainable Cities,* identified
global urbanization trends and broad ways to address their challenges
to achieve sustainability.

Following this, Condon's *Seven Rules for Sustainable Communities*
(2010) identifies specific actions communities can undertake, including restoring streetcar cities; designing interconnected street systems;
locating commercial services, frequent transit, and schools within a
five-minute walk; locating good jobs close to affordable homes; providing a diversity of housing types; and creating a linked system of natural areas and parks. Doing so, Condon says, will lead to more healthy
and less polluting cities, important goals especially in the age of climate change.

Speaking of climate change, Russell's *The Agile City* (2011) argues
that improving building energy efficiency through such efforts as the

US Green Building Council's LEED scoring system, and changing transportation systems to meet emerging market demands can reduce greenhouse gas emissions more than tax incentives and massive alternative energy investments. In *Urbanism in the Age of Climate Change*, Calthorpe (2010) argues that these and other efforts must be conducted at a regional scale to be truly effective.

Farr (2007) argues in *Sustainable Urbanism* that American metropolitan areas need to increase residential density; integrate transportation and land use; create sustainable neighborhoods that include housing choice, car-free areas, locally owned stores, walkable neighborhoods, and broad accessibility; design communities to advance the health and environmental benefits of linking humans to nature, including opportunities to walk to open spaces; and facilitate construction of high-performance buildings and district energy systems.

*Creating Healthier Communities*

Frank et al. (2003), in *Health and Community Design*, were among the first to examine the relationship between urban form and public health. In *Urban Sprawl and Public Health*, Frumkin et al. (2004) extends this genre, showing how sprawling development patterns affect public health. They outlines strategies for improving public health through alternative design, land use, and transportation approaches. In *Making Healthy Places*, Dannenberg et al. (2011) shows how community design affects health, discusses how the built environment influences health, and offers strategies for creating healthier communities. Jackson's *Designing Healthy Communities* (2012) offers specific planning and design approaches to link sustainability and public health through community design.

*Tear Up the Parking Lot, Rebuild Paradise*

The refrain in Joni Mitchell's 1970 hit "Big Yellow Taxi" was "They paved paradise and put up a parking lot," speaking broadly to urban expansion on Hawai'i. This refrain is now being turned on its head as suburbs reshape themselves. With apologies to Mitchell, the new refrain might just be, "Tear up a parking lot, rebuild paradise."

A growing body of work focuses on infill, redevelopment, and reuse of suburban landscapes. Schmitz (2003) may have been the first to argue comprehensively for the role of suburban areas in reshaping America. In *The New Shape of Suburbia* this author contends that closer-in suburban nodes and commercial strips offer important transportation advantages and can lead to more efficient use of infrastructure. Schmitz also identifies opportunities to revitalize neighborhoods and in doing so advance green development. Peiser at al. (2007) expands on these themes through a series of case studies in *Regenerating Older Suburbs*. In *Retrofitting Suburbia*, Dunham-Jones and Williamson (2009) present numerous design options to convert parking lots and low-intensity commercial strips and centers into mixed-use developments, especially in suburban areas. A specialized version of this genre is Christensen's *Big Box Reuse* (2008), in which numerous examples are given of converting retail big boxes into a variety of public and nonprofit uses. These are especially important interim uses between when retail occupants abandon the space and when the local market has gelled enough to warrant redevelopment of the site.

The problem is that it remains more difficult to recycle parking lots than build new subdivisions in greenfields. The approach pursued in Nashville includes four overarching principles in redeveloping commercial corridors that are mostly parking lots (Urban Land Institute 2010a, 9):

- Provide complete transportation options with choices for pedestrians, cyclists, transit users, and individual autos.
- Support surrounding neighborhoods with housing and services in a pedestrian-friendly environment.
- Encourage infill to use existing infrastructure and maximize transit opportunities.
- Be flexible given the existing and evolving economic realities.

Communities can become YIMBY (yes in my backyard) supporters instead of NIMBY (not in my backyard) opponents if they see the following benefits and are allowed to participate in the process leading to parking lot redevelopment. First, redeveloping parking lots, usually along commercial corridors, diverts pressure away from redeveloping neighborhoods themselves. Second, the community must have constructive participation in the redevelopment design. Third, if a transit option is part of large-scale, corridor-based redevelopment, the community needs to be engaged constructively in its planning as well. Fourth, credible information is needed to show how their property values will be affected. Studies consistently show the effect will be positive.

## Transit and TODs

Several works address the role of transit and especially TODs in reshaping metropolitan America. Perhaps the leader of this genre is Cervero's *The Transit Metropolis* (1998). This book, written just as America's light-rail systems were being launched and before bus rapid transit systems became popular, demonstrates how other countries planned and designed those systems to enhance economic development, improve social equity, and advance sustainability. In *The New Transit Town*, Dittmar and Ohland (2003) devise a taxonomy of TODs based on different contexts and scales; outline the planning, policy, and regulatory framework of "successful" projects; identify obstacles to financing and strategies for overcoming them; address issues relating to traffic and parking; and pose performance measures to assess outcomes. In *Developing Around Transit*, Dunphy et al. (2005) offers planning, design, and financial strategies for successful TOD development. Altoon and Auld's (2011) *Urban Transformations* go into more detail in providing numerous case studies on the planning and design of transit stations, TODs, and transit-adjacent developments in the United States and other countries.

## Reforming Land Use Regulation

Land use regulation, for good or bad, is how we manage our land resources. To change our built landscapes we need to change our regulatory mechanisms. In *A Legal Guide to Urban and Sustainable Development for Planners, Developers, and Architects*, Slone et al. (2008)

acquaint practitioners with the tools needed to achieve desired sustainability outcomes within the constraints of existing codes. Freilich and White (2008), in *21st Century Land Development Code*, go further by offering a framework for reforming (mostly) suburban development codes to facilitate sustainability, traditional neighborhood development, TOD, and mixed-use centers, among other development options. Getting down to a specific kind of reform, in *Form-Based Codes*, Parolek et al. (2008), show how this specific alternative to zoning can reshape the built landscape in ways that are more sustainable.

The overall message is that America's communities need to make it easier than it is now to build infill and redevelopment projects, mixed-use projects, and projects with mixed-housing options.

These and other works are mostly about planning and design, and regulatory implementation. I will now introduce other areas of reform needed to reshape America; they will not be easy.

## (NOT SO EASY) POLICIES TO RESHAPE AMERICA

The initiatives I outlined above are possible only with changes in regulations and decision-making processes, probably combined. For instance, the benefits of converting parking lots, dead or dying commercial strips, and retail malls into mixed-used developments served by bus rapid transit, streetcar, or light-rail systems may seem logical, but NIMBY opposition may foil these opportunities. The solution may be coordinated public education and engagement (see Lennertz and Lutzenhiser 2006). Williamson (2013) offers especially important perspectives.

What if we could change the tools and institutions to be responsive to market preferences? In my view, this would require federal and/or state legislation to make markets more efficient and responsive to needs. The bottom line is that by allowing the market to meet needs without undue inducements leading to inefficient decisions by builders, buyers, and policy makers, America can be more prosperous in 2030 than now.

In ascending order of difficulty to implement, I offer eight recommendations.

*Make Accessory Dwelling Units Legal*

Accessory dwelling units (ADUs) are complete residential units with their own entry and living quarters on the same property as a primary residence (such as a unit over a garage or stand-alone structure), attached to the primary unit (such as a small townhouse), or within the primary home itself (in the attic, basement, or section of the main living area). For millions of seniors who want to age in place as long as they can, ADUs offer them this option by reducing the living space they need and adding a companion to the property for social, caregiving and security purposes. For people out of college or in the midst of life changes (such as losing a job, partner, or even family), ADUs are an attractive alternative to apartments, which may not be located near their social networks or jobs. ADUs also enable home owners to earn supplemental income. The trouble is that most zoning codes in most communities in the United States forbid them, fearing overparking on streets, adding criminal elements to the neighborhood, overtaxing public facilities, and generally moving the neighborhood toward blight. These and other myths seem to dominate the public debate (Chapple et al. 2012). I estimate that if every American community had the kind of reasoned ADU policy advocated by the American Association of Retired Persons (Cobb and Dvorak 2000), by 2030 about 10 percent or more of the then 243 million American households could live in one; these would be mostly seniors, young individuals, couples starting out in life, and those in major life stage changes.

*Eliminate Social Engineering through the Federal Tax Code*

The federal tax code subsidizes home ownership in ways that overvalue owner-occupied property and undervalue renter-occupied property. Through tax breaks and guarantees, the Congressional Budget Office (2009) estimates that subsidies for homeownership, including the mortgage interest deduction, were $230 billion in 2009, but were only $60 billion for programs aiding renters. According to economic reasoning, subsidies artificially increase value. If there were no subsidies, home ownership would decline, renting would increase, and development patterns would be more compact and less costly to serve. We might not be able to change federal home ownership subsidies but by raising renter-based subsidies to be on par, at least the playing field would be leveled. As it is, the tax code induces more people to buy homes than rent, possibly making them more vulnerable to economic hardship. This could be called social engineering, leading to those with fewer economic endowments subsidizing those with more.

*Eliminate Social Engineering through State Property Tax Mechanisms*

State tax codes typically confer property tax benefits for owner-occupied property more favorably than for renter-occupied property, chiefly through homestead exemptions or by assessing owner-occupied property a lower property tax rate than rental property. This is because apartments are often considered "commercial," as if people were commodities. The effect is that renters end up subsidizing owners. This could also be called social engineering, again leading to those with fewer economic endowments subsidizing those with more (Blais 2010).

*Level the Home Purchase Playing Field*

In terms of construction costs, space use, and energy consumption, one of the most efficient home owner options is condominiums. Yet federal underwriting institutions discriminate against them. A key element of housing finance is the ability of the developer or the developer's financier to sell mortgage "paper" to the secondary market. This is routine when it comes to the buyer of a single-family home. But when it comes to condominiums, federal underwriting requires between 50 percent and 70 percent of the entire project to be sold to owner-occupants before government-sponsored enterprises such as Fannie Mae or Freddie Mac may purchase the mortgage paper for the entire project. In my view, such practices should be eliminated and condominium ownership needs to be encouraged. Otherwise, we are simply socially engineering people away from the option many prefer.

*Eliminate Social Engineering through Local Exclusionary Zoning*

Thousands of suburban jurisdictions use zoning to prevent lower and moderate income households from moving into them. Most of the more than one hundred Atlanta metropolitan suburban jurisdictions do not allow attached housing, small lots, or small homes (Nelson 2001). The effect is to use zoning to socially engineer suburbia to steer lower income, usually minority households into the few jurisdictions that allow higher density housing and away from others. From Anthony Downs' *Open Up the Suburbs* (1973) to Jonathan Levine's *Zoned Out* (2005), we know what needs to be done, we just have to do it.

*Eliminate the Requirement to Drive until You Qualify*

Housing economics is essentially based on the cost of housing plus the cost of location. However, we use federal regulations to ignore location costs. For people wishing to buy homes, federally-inspired underwriting regulations require that housing expenses not exceed about 30 percent of the household budget. Transportation costs are not included in this calculation. Nationally, about 50 percent of the typical American family income is spent on housing and transportation, with about 28 percent spent on housing. If a location cuts transportation costs to about 10 percent, the household would be no worse off if it bought a home at a location that absorbs 40 percent of the household budget. Alas, mortgage underwriting conventions prevent the household from buying into a low transportation-cost location, forcing it to incur higher transportation costs to find a location where the house price exclusive of transportation costs qualifies for a mortgage. It is called "drive until you qualify" and is a recipe for financial disaster. We need mortgage instruments that recognize the housing value benefits of centrality, land use connectivity, and multimodalism.

## Instill Fair Facility Financing

Most local governments finance public facility capital and operating costs through average cost approaches. Although this has the advantage of being simple, the result is that less costly areas pay more than their full cost and more costly areas pay less than theirs. This "subsidy" from low-cost to high-cost areas induces more high-cost development and stifles low-cost development, with the result that average costs increase over time, thus forcing higher taxes and rates on everyone. This approach also provides a financial incentive for the underutilization of existing facilities and reduced efficiency. The scheme is not economically sustainable.

Consider an example involving fire stations. Assume the locally preferred level of service is a five-minute response time. Consider also that each fire station costs the same to build and about two million dollars per year to operate. Suppose there are two fire stations each located to achieve the five-minute response time. Total annual costs are four million dollars. One fire station serves eight thousand homes in an area that cannot grow because of local zoning. It costs two hundred fifty dollars per year to serve each home. The other fire station serves two thousand homes in a low-density area also unable to grow because of local zoning, so it costs one thousand dollars per year to serve each home. Assume the average assessed value per unit is the same. All ten thousand homes pay an average of four hundred dollars per year. Homes in the low-cost area pay 60 percent more than their full cost, while homes in the high-cost area pay only 40 percent of theirs. The effect of this subsidy from low-cost to high-cost areas is to induce more high-cost sprawled development and discourage more low-cost infill development. If another ten thousand homes were added, serving the same density as the high-cost area, five more fire stations would be needed. Total costs would rise to fourteen million dollars and each of the twenty thousand homes would pay seven hundred dollars. Economists call the result inefficient. Research shows that, over time, the outcome would be fewer jobs and lower incomes than what would have resulted from more efficient development patterns.

There is another consideration: equity. Often, low-cost areas are those occupied by lower income households. If there is a subsidy from lower cost areas to higher cost ones, it may be that lower income households are implicitly subsidizing higher income households, which is an inequitable outcome. In my view, public facility pricing schemes need to be reworked to eliminate the costly and inefficient outcomes to current pricing schemes, especially when they are inequitable.

### Instill Permitting Discipline

America built several million more homes during the 2000s than the market could absorb. In economics, more supply relative to demand depresses prices. One wonders whether the magnitude of the Great Recession would have been less, with many more millions of Americans employed and federal deficits much lower, had there been just enough new residential units permitted to meet demand. Whether it is private trade associations or government agencies or a combination, some entity is needed to instill discipline in local governments to prevent issuing permits in excess demand.

## THE OPPORTUNITY TO RESHAPE METROPOLITAN AMERICA

These may be challenging propositions. However, progress is being made. When I began my planning practice in the early 1970s, planned unit developments and cluster housing were seen as innovations. It is now difficult to keep track of all the innovations that have occurred since then. Thankfully, several organizations provide details of them, often including case studies and practice guides, with the effect that the capacity of local governments to respond to emerging market demands is greatly enhanced. I recommend especially the tool-based smart growth websites of such organizations as the US Environmental Protection Agency,[2] US Department of Housing and Urban Development,[3] National Association of Realtors,[4] Smart Growth America,[5] Reconnecting America,[6] Center for Neighborhood Technology,[7] Center for Transit-Oriented Development,[8] and the organizations with which these groups are affiliated.

The progress may seem slow because even in a banner development year new development accounts for only a percentage point or two of existing development. Extended over time, change can be substantial. That is why I am optimistic that most new development to 2030 may indeed occur as infill and redevelopment, and as mixed-use, higher density, master-planned development within urbanized metropolitan areas.

Thomas (2010), for instance, found that new residential construction in the fifty largest metropolitan areas is shifting into infill and redevelopment area. Between the 1990s and late 2000s, the average share of new residential units built in those areas increased from 17 percent to 25 percent. More dramatic rates of change have occurred in such metropolitan areas as New York City (15 percent to 63 percent), Chicago (7 percent to 45 percent), Portland (9 percent to 38 percent), Denver (5 percent to 32 percent), Kansas City (12 percent to 27 percent), Seattle (11 percent to 31 percent), Milwaukee (6 percent to 25 percent), and Los Angeles (11 percent to 25 percent). If continued, these trends suggest that more than half of all new development would occur in infill and redevelopment areas by 2030 and another large share, perhaps nearly all, would occur in the suburban areas surrounding them.

Given the new economy combined with changing demographics, market forces, and emerging preferences, there is much to do. Those metropolitan areas that take advantage of these opportunities will be the winners of the twenty-first century.

# Notes

INTRODUCTION

1. Figures for 1900–2000 from www.census.gov/hhes/www/housing/census/historic/owner.html; estimate for 2010 by the author based on trends since 2008 reported in www.census.gov/hhes/www/housing/hvs/hvs.html.

2. Adapted from Kim (2007).

3. This is based on my analysis of the raw National Association of Realtors survey data. For details, see chapter 1.

4. Calculated from the American Housing Survey for 2009 (2011). www.huduser.org/portal/datasets/ahs/ahsdata09.html.

5. These calculations are based on the National Household Travel Survey for 1995, 2001, and 2009. See http://nhts.ornl.gov/.

6. This analysis based on data from www.zillow.com.


CHAPTER 1

1. Historical Census of Housing Tables Ownership Rates, www.census.gov/hhes/www/housing/census/historic/ownrate.html.

2. Housing vacancies and home ownership for 2005, www.census.gov/hhes/www/housing/hvs/annual05/ann05t13.html.

3. The coefficient of determination (R2) is 0.78; the t-ratio is 5.26; and $p > 0.01$.

4. See also Steiner 2009.

5. For brevity, "Hispanic" means Latino with all racial combinations such as Asian, black, and white Hispanic.

6. See The Nation's Report Card produced by the National Assessment of Educational Progress of the US Department of Education, www.nces.ed.gov/nationsreportcard/pdf/main2008/2009479.pdf.

7. See "Average wealth by wealth class 2009," accessed July 14, 2012, from stateofworkingamerica.org/charts/average-wealth-by-wealth-class-in-2009/.

8. Ibid.

9. For an extensive review of the Great Recession causes, see Faiola et al. 2008.

10. Considering that there were about 75 million home owners in 2010, losing 5 million would reduce the home ownership rate from above 66 percent to about 60 percent—a rate not seen since 1960.

11. See "Lawmakers Join Industry Groups to Urge Revising Minimum 20% Down Requirement," accessed July 14, 2012, at http://www.nahb.org/news_details .aspx?newsID=12938&fromGSA=1

12. See *American Housing Survey of the United States 2009,* table 3-14, www .census.gov/housing/ahs/data/ahs2009.html.

13. See Ford, "Five Myths about the American Dream," *Washington Post,* November 10, 2011, accessed July 14, 2012, at www.washingtonpost.com/opinions /five-myths-about-the-american-dream/2011/11/10/gIQAP4t0eP_story.html.

14. See NAHB/Wells Fargo Housing Opportunity Index: Complete History by Metropolitan Area, www.nahb.org/reference_list.aspx?sectionID=135, and compare national average sales prices in 2000 to 2011 prices using the consumer price index calculator, www.data.bls.gov/cgi-bin/cpicalc.pl?cost1=1&year1=2000&year2 =2011.

15. From Housing and Household Economic Statistics Division, Census Bureau, www.census.gov/hhes/www/housing/hvs/qtr111/files/q111press.pdf.

16. I am grateful to Woods & Poole, Economics, Inc. (2011) for permission to use some of its data, especially population, household, and employment projections to 2030. For population projections, it uses a standard cohort-component analysis based on fertility and mortality in each county in the United States. In addition, total population "demand" is based on employment projections such that if labor demand increases for a particular county then either the labor force participation rate will increase or population in-migration will make up the difference, with the inverse also used as needed. Thus, future county migration based on population by age, sex, and race is attributable to employment opportunities. There are two exceptions: population aged sixty-five and older and college and military-aged population are based on historical net migration patterns and not economic conditions. The integration of economic and demographic analysis is a particularly attractive element of the Woods & Poole projection approach.

17. Figures for individual metropolitan areas are available online from Island Press at www.ReshapeMetroAmerica.org.

18. New Strategist uses the term iGeneration for those born after 1994, which they call the Millennials. Their profile of the iGeneration is found at http://www.new strategist.com/store/index.cfm/product/307_7/the-millennials-americans-born-1977 -to-1994-5th-ed-hardcover.cfm

19. See Households by Type and Size: 1900 to 2002, www.census.gov/statab /hist/HS-12.pdf.

20. US Census Bureau, Current Population Survey, 2010 Annual Social and Economic Supplement, table AVG1 "Average Number of People per Household, by Race and Hispanic Origin, Marital Status, Age, and Education of Householder: 2010," accessed July 14, 2012, at www.census.gov/population/www/socdemo/hh-fam/cps 2010.html.

CHAPTER 2

1. See Pew Research Report, October 2009, College Enrollment Hits All-Time High, pewsocialtrends.org/files/2010/10/college-enrollment.pdf.

2. Senior housing includes several types, such as senior apartments (being studio and room units designed for senior needs but usually not included in a continuous-care senior complex), independent living (which includes on-call medical assistance, meal plan options, and other support services), nursing homes, and memory care (for seniors in various stages of dementia).

3. See table AVG1. Average Number of People per Household, by Race and Hispanic Origin, Marital Status, Age, and Education of Householder: 2011 US Census Bureau, accessed February 21, 2012, www.census.gov/population/www/socdemo/hh-fam/cps2011.html.

4. Analysis of Census SF-3 data based on HCT7. See also Myers and Ryu (2008) on changing propensities to buy and sell by five-year age cohort, noting that after sixty-five, such households have a higher propensity to sell than to buy.

5. What constitutes "walkability" is beyond the scope of this book, but generally it is maximizing destinations from an origin with minimum barriers. For measuring walkability, see Michael et al. (2009).

6. Porter Novelli is a public relations company based in Washington, DC www.porternovelli.com. We use their data with permission.

7. These categories are based substantially on work by Myers and Ryu (2008). They suggest that households have a constantly declining propensity to relocate from the mid-thirties into the mid-fifties. The people in the group age thirty-five to fifty-four are established in their careers, have growing families, and have more or less settled in their communities. For the most part, people in the age group fifty-five to sixty-nine are empty nesters at the peak of their earning power and the least likely to move from their current residence among all the age groups. Unlike other analysts, whose cut off for seniors is sixty-five years, I use seventy years. The principal reason is that Myers and Ryu's work (2008) showed that after decades of relative stability in their home situation, the propensity to relocate increases substantially around age seventy and accelerates. This is the time when empty nesters downsize, sometimes several times in their remaining lifetime.

8. US Bureau of the Census, www.census.gov/population/www/projections/summarytables.html.

9. Assuming 2.5 persons per household.

10. US Census Bureau and US HUD (2011), *American Housing Survey for the United States: 2009*, table 2-8. Neighborhood-Occupied Units, compared to table 1-1, including interpolation. Accessed July 23, 2012, from www.census.gov/housing/ahs/data/national.html

11. Assuming each household occupies its own dwelling.

12. Research indicates that eight units per acre is the minimum density needed to support regular transit services. See Parsons Brinckerhoff Quade and Douglas, Inc. (1996) and Cervero and Seskin (1995).

13. See Parsons Brinckerhoff Quade and Douglas, Inc. (1996) and Cervero and Seskin (1995).

14. For instance, an analysis of Zillow.com home values in metropolitan Atlanta between the mid-2000s and early 2010s found that homes in the farthest suburbs, dominated by large-acreage lots, lost about half their value. Closer-in suburbs where lots are smaller but are still one-quarter to one-half acre in size lost about 40 percent of their value. Homes within the I-285 perimeter freeway, dominated by small lots and attached products, lost about 30 percent of their value. The same database indicates that home values where smaller lots dominate were rebounding but continued to soften farther out.

15. See *New York Times*, March 3, 2012, "As Young Lose Interest in Cars, G.M. Turns to MTV for Help," www.nytimes.com/2012/03/23/business/media/to-draw -reluctant-young-buyers-gm-turns-to-mtv.html?pagewanted=all.


## CHAPTER 3

1. See www.census.gov/statab/hist/HS-12.pdf, "Households by Type and Size: 1900 to 2002."

2. See table HH-6. Average Population Per Household and Family: 1940 to Present, accessed July 24, 2012, www.census.gov/population/socdemo/hh-fam /tabHH-6.pdf.

3. See J. Phillips, R. Beasley, and A. Rodgers (2005). District of Columbia Population and Housing Trends. Washington, DC: City of Washington, DC, accessed July 24, 2012,http://www.neighborhoodinfodc.org/pdfs/demographic_trends05.pdf.

4. So-called subprime mortgages required no income documentation or proof of ability to support a mortgage, and lenient credit scores (if any), combined with very low adjustable rate mortgages that would start at around 3.5 percent but climb rapidly based on certain formulas and indices.

5. See HH-6. Average Population Per Household and Family: 1940 to Present, accessed July 24, 2012, www.census.gov/population/socdemo/hh-fam/hh6.xls.

6. I take the share of households by age group with children in 2010 and multiply it by the share of households in 2030 for each age group, sum, and derive the overall share of households with children.

7. These include independent living units, often 1- or 2-bedroom units with a kitchen, in senior complexes that are akin to apartments but with meal service, organized activities, and medical assistance, if needed; assisted living with a higher degree of medical attention and typically smaller units but without kitchens; nursing units often with more than one person per unit; and memory care for those in need of special assistance due to dementia.

8. See Vacation-Home Sales Up in 2009 but Investment Sales Down, accessed July 24, 2012, www.resortlife.blogs.realtor.org/2010/04/12/vacation-home-sales-up -but-investment-home-sales-down/.

9. Using the quarterly Housing Vacancy Survey (www.census.gov/history /www/programs/housing/housing_vacancy_survey.html) to estimate the normal housing vacancy rates between 1990 and 2005, I estimate the excess housing in 2010 to range between about 2.5 million and about 4.5 million units, depending on assumptions relating to owners and renters, and seasonal units. Using the persons per housing unit in 2000 to estimate demand in 2010 falls within this range.

10. See Historical Census of Housing Tables: Homeownership by Selected Demographic and Housing Characteristics, accessed July 24, 2012,www.census.gov /hhes/www/housing/census/historic/ownerchar.html.

11. See table 14. Homeownership Rates by Area: 1960 to 2008, accessed July 24, 2012, from www.census.gov/hhes/www/housing/hvs/annual08/ann08t14 .xls. This figure is based on a different sampling methodology than the decennial census and typically reports a higher home ownership rate than does that census. For instance, the decennial census figure for 2000 is 66.2 percent while this source reports a rate of 67.4 percent. Because of systemic overestimations between the 2000 and 2010 censuses a peak rate of 67.8 percent in 2005 might be more realistic.

12. I recommend the *Washington Post's* articles in the series "The Crash: What Went Wrong?," www.washingtonpost.com/wp-srv/business/risk/, including What Went Wrong, October 15, 2008 accessed July 24, 2012, from http://www.washington post.com/wp-dyn/content/article/2008/10/14/AR2008101403343.html; Banking Regulator Played Advocate, November 23, 2008, accessed July 24, 2012, http://www .washingtonpost.com/wp-dyn/content/article/2008/11/22/AR2008112202213 .html; and The Frenzy, December 16, 2008, accessed July 24, 2012, http://www .washingtonpost.com/wp-dyn/content/article/2008/12/15/AR2008121503561.html. http://www.washingtonpost.com/wp-srv/business/risk/

13. See Pendall et al., *Demographic Challenges and Opportunities for U.S. Housing Markets,* www.urban.org/publications/412520.html, who arrived at a middle projection of 63.3 percent home ownership by 2030.

14. See also Leinberger (2010).

15. An alternative to foreclosure is through short sales, in which the lender writes down (reduces) the mortgage balance, the investor acquires the home, and the former owner either leaves or rents it back.

16. See "Private Equity's Foreclosures for Rentals Net 8%," *Bloomberg Markets,* www.bloomberg.com/news/2012-03-13/private-equity-buying-u-s-foreclosures-for -hot-rentals-net-8-mortgages.html.

17. There is no inventory of communities allowing ADUs. Over nearly 40 years, my professional and academic work has allowed me to become knowledgeable of hundreds of cities across the United States, but I find it is the rare community that allows ADUs, and most of them tend to be central cities. Despite reviewing hundreds of them over my career, I have yet to see home owner association documents allow retrofit ADUs. The exception are some new urbanism communities that included ADUs explicitly in the construction of selected units, but even in those communities, retrofit ADUs added to existing units may be problematic.

18. The Regulatory Barriers Clearinghouse provides numerous and growing examples of successful ADU approaches. See www.huduser.org/rbc/newsletter/vol6 iss2more.html.

19. This is based on data reported in the *American Housing Survey* over the period 1985 to 2009. See www.census.gov/housing/ahs/.

20. For instance, see "Animal McMansion," *New York Times,* Nov. 13, 2011, www.nytimes.com/2011/11/13/us/homework-and-jacuzzis-as-dorms-move-to -mcmansions-in-california.html?pagewanted=all. See also "Parallel Universe: College Students in Merced, CA Rent Underwater McMansions, Saving Money, Annoying Neighbors" in Huffington Post, http://www.huntingtonnews.net/13351.

## CHAPTER 4

1. The Energy Information Administration of the US Department of Energy conducts a periodic stratified random sample called Commercial Buildings Energy Consumption Survey of all nonindustrial buildings in the nation. Total space in 1992 was 69.7 billion square feet, and for 2003 it was 71.7 billion square feet, or an average of 233 and 246 square feet per person for populations of 256.5 million and 290.8 million, respectively.

2. See Telework Research Network, "How Many People Telecommute?" www.teleworkresearchnetwork.com/people-telecommute.

3. See US Department of Transportation, Federal Highway Administration, Working At Home—The Quiet Revolution, NHTS Brief, July 2008, http://nhts.ornl.gov/briefs/Working%20at%20Home.pdf.

4. See US Government Accountability Office, "Continuity of Operations: Agencies Could Improve Planning for Use of Alternative Facilities and Telework During Disruptions," May 2006, www.gao.gov/new.items/d06740t.pdf.

5. See "The top 10 telecommuting traps" www.codefez.com/the-top-10-telecommuting-traps/.

6. See "New GartnerGroup Report from Gartner Direct Aims to Reduce IT Total Cost of Ownership." *Business Wire.* New York: Feb. 4, 1999.

7. See *Wall Street Journal,* "Corporate Cram Bedevils Office Recovery," Feb. 29, 2012, accessed July 24, 2012, www.online.wsj.com/article/SB10001424052970203833004577250050812013624.html.

8. See CoreNet Global news release, Feb. 28, 2012, "Office Space Per Worker Will Drop to 100 Square Feet or Below for Many Companies Within Five Years," www.corenetglobal.org/files/home/info_center/global_press_releases/pdf/pr120227_office space.pdf.

9. CoStar conducts ongoing research to produce and maintain a comprehensive database of commercial real estate information for US markets. See their website at http://www.costar.com/.

10. The US Census Bureau, Annual Survey of Manufactures, produces annual estimates of e-commerce activity. My focus is on e-commerce retail sales. For e-commerce activity in 1998 and 1999, see table 4 in the summary of the Annual Survey of Manufactures for 1998 and 1999, accessed July 24, 2012, from www.census.gov/econ/estats/1998/1999_1998tables.pdf.

11. For more information about US retail trade, total and e-commerce sales: 1999 and 2000, see www.census.gov/econ/estats/2000/table5.pdf.

12. US Census Bureau News, May 17, 2012, Quarterly retail e-commerce sales, 1st quarter 2012, www.census.gov/retail/mrts/www/data/pdf/ec_current.pdf.

13. One projection has e-commerce accounting for more than 20 percent of retail sales by 2020. However, the source also projected such sales would account for nearly 6 percent of all retail sales by 2012, but the actual figure was less than 5 percent. G. Maguire. E-commerce: A statistical market analysis and forecast of emerging trends. www.csustan.edu/honors/documents/journals/crossings/Maguire.pdf.

14. See L. Heller, April 20, 2011, "The Future of Online Shopping: 10 Trends to Watch," *Forbes,* www.forbes.com/sites/lauraheller/2011/04/20/the-future-of-online-shopping-10-trends-to-watch/.

15. www.eia.gov/emeu/cbecs/cbecs2003/detailed_tables_2003/detailed_tables _2003.html.

16. www.eia.gov/emeu/mecs/mecs2006/2006tables.html.

17. See Marshall & Swift, *Marshall Valuation Service* (2010). Marshall & Swift provide an appraisal guide for developing replacement costs and depreciated values of buildings and other improvements. For details, see their website at www.marshall swift.com/

18. See Commercial Buildings Energy Consumption Survey for 2003. US Department of Energy, Energy Information Administration, accessed July 24, 2012, www.eia.gov/emeu/cbecs/cbecs2003/detailed_tables_2003/detailed_tables_2003 .html.


## CHAPTER 5

1. See Commercial Buildings Energy Consumption Survey for 2003, www.eia .gov/emeu/cbecs/cbecs2003/detailed_tables_2003/detailed_tables_2003.html.

2. See the National Trust for Historic Preservation, www.preservationnation .org/.


## CHAPTER 6

1. Tu and Eppli (1999) compared resale prices for the Andrew Duany–designed Kentlands new urbanism development in Gaithersburg, Maryland, during the mid-1990s. Data from Zillow.com indicate that between 2007—the peak of home resale prices—and 2011—perhaps the ebb of values—property values in the Kentlands zip code fell 15 percent compared to 35 percent in the other Gaithersburg zip codes.

2. The firm Walk Score (www.walkscore.com) uses an algorithm that is based on walking distances from an address to a diverse set of nearby amenities. Certain categories are weighted more heavily than others to reflect destinations associated with more walking trips. In addition, road connectivity metrics such as intersection density and average block length are factored into the score.

3. These figures are adapted from the Economic Research Service of the US Department of Agriculture for major land uses (see www.ers.usda.gov/data/Major LandUses/). I report only developed land less rural roads. In 2007, urban land plus rural residential areas comprised 164 million acres or more than 12 percent of all privately owned land, much of it invading some of the nation's most highly productive agricultural land, especially in California and Florida.

4. Benefits include flood control, biodiversity, biomass fuel production, food production, air and water cleansing, recreation and social spaces, exercise that can reduce body mass and improve public health, and capitalized amenity values.

5. The original figure was about $4,000 per acre for 1995, which I have adjusted to 2012 dollars.

6. Marks (2011) would have no discount; that is, one would multiply $6,000 by 100 years, resulting in a present value of $600,000 per acre of undeveloped open

space. Cowan (2001) would even anticipate a positive discount rate, which would make the future discounted value higher still.

7. See US Energy Information Administration, Annual Energy Review, www .eia.gov/totalenergy/data/annual/index.cfm.

8. See US Energy Information Administration, Oil Crude and Petroleum Products, Explained, Data & Statistics, www.eia.gov/energyexplained/index.cfm?page =oil_home#tab2.

9. See US Department of Energy, Energy Efficiency Trends in Residential and Commercial Buildings, 2008, http://apps1.eere.energy.gov/buildings/publications /pdfs/corporate/bt_stateindustry.pdf.

10. Alternatively, the energy consumed per square foot increases. However, the appropriate impact measure is per person.

11. Calculated from the American Housing Survey for the United States, 2009, table 1-3, www.census.gov/housing/ahs/data/national.html.

12. In 2010, the Bureau of Economic Analysis reported that there were a total of 174 million jobs in the United States. See www.bea.gov/regional/index.htm.

13. For jobs lost in 2008, see www.bea.gov/regional/index.htm.

14. Figures adjusted from 1997 to 2012 using the Consumer Price Index. Employment figures are from www.bea.gov/regional/index.htm.

15. See Bureau of Economic Analysis, Regional Economic Accounts, www.bea .gov/regional/index.htm.

16. Woods & Poole Economics (2011) projects about 223.6 million total jobs in 2030.

17. The unemployment rate in 2030 can not be known. However, if it were to be about 6.0 percent, given business-as-usual development patterns, directing all new growth into existing developed areas could reduce the unemployment rate to about 4.8 percent—a 20 percent reduction.

18. Adapted from Voith (1998).

19. See T. Tritch, 2012. "Still Crawling Out of a Very Deep Hole," *New York Times*, April 7, www.nytimes.com/2012/04/08/opinion/sunday/still-crawling-out-of-a -very-deephole.html?scp=17&sq=april%208,%202012&st=Search.

20. See P. Langdon, 2012. "Suburban housing recovery? Perhaps not in our lifetime, expert says." Better Cities & Towns, March 28, www.bettercities.net/news -opinion/links/17687/suburban-housing-recovery-perhaps-not-our-lifetime-expert -says.

21. See Housing tenure and type of area, US Bureau of Labor Statistics, www .bls.gov/cex/2010/Standard/tenure.pdf.

22. See H&T Affordability Index, Center for Neighborhood Technology, http://htaindex.cnt.org/.

23. This is calculated as the sum of foreclosure notices, proceedings, and real estate owned by the lender.

24. This is an area of ongoing research by my colleagues and me at the Metropolitan Research Center at the University of Utah.

25. See Board of Governors of the Federal Reserve System, Troubled Asset Relief Program (TARP) Information, www.federalreserve.gov/bankinforeg/tarpinfo.htm.

26. See US Bureau of Labor Statistics, Consumer Expenditures, 2010, www .bls.gov/news.release/cesan.nr0.htm. See also written testimony of Secretary of Hous-

ing and Urban Development Shaun Donovan on March 18, 2009, www.hud
.gov/offices/cir/test090318.cfm. For a broader discussion, see Surface Transportation
Planning Process (2005).

## CHAPTER 7

1. Robbie Whelan, 2012, "What's Next for Housing? More Sprawl," *The Wall Street Journal*, June 14, http://blogs.wsj.com/developments/2012/06/14/whats-next-for-housing-more-sprawl/.

2. Smart Growth, www.epa.gov/dced/.

3. Sustainable Housing and Communities, portal.hud.gov/hudportal/HUD?src=/program_offices/sustainable_housing_communities.

4. Smart Growth Program, www.realtor.org/programs/smart-growth-program.

5. www.smartgrowthamerica.org/.

6. www.reconnectingamerica.org/.

7. www.cnt.org/.

8. www.ctod.org/.

# References and Selected Bibliography

AARP Public Policy Institute (1997). *Community Transportation Survey.* Association of Retired Persons, Washington, DC.

Adams, J. T. (1931). *The Epic of America.* New York: Little.

Altoon, R. A., and J. C. Auld (2011). *Urban Transformations: Transit-Oriented Development and the Sustainable City.* Mumbai, India: Images.

ARA National Seniors Housing Group (2011). *2011 Seniors Industry Outlook.* Dallas, TX. Accessed February 21, 2012, http://www.arausa.com/FTP/seniors/ARA%202011%20White%20Paper.pdf.

Arora, A. (2007). *Inventory of Policies Affecting Parking within the NYMTC Region.* New Brunswick, NJ: Bloustein School of Planning and Public Policy, Rutgers University.

Baldasarre, M. (2001, 2002). *PPIC Statewide Survey: Special Survey on Land Use.* San Francisco: Public Policy Institute of California.

Bartholomew, K., and R. Ewing (2011). Hedonic price effects of pedestrian- and transit-oriented development. *Journal of Planning Literature* 26 (1): 18–34.

Bartholomew, K., A. C. Nelson, and G. Meakins (2011). *Envisioning Efficiency: How Scenario Planning Can Lead to More Cost-Effective Transportation Investments.* Washington, DC: Transportation for America.

Belden Russonello & Stewart Research and Communications (2004). *2004 American Community Survey: National Survey on Communities Conducted for Smart Growth America and National Association of Realtors.* Washington, DC: National Association of Realtors.

———. (2011). *Community Preference Survey.* Washington, DC: National Association of Realtors. (Cited in text as NAR 2011.)

Bettencourt, L. M. A., J. Lobo, D. Helbing, C. Kuhnert, G. B. West (2007). Growth, innovation, scaling, and the pace of life in cities. *Proceedings of the National Academy of Sciences* 104 (17): 7301–7306.

Blais, Pamela (2010). *Perverse Cities: Hidden Subsidies, Wonky Policy, and Urban Sprawl.* Vancouver, BC: UBC Press.

Bruegmann, R. (2005). *Sprawl: A Compact History.* Chicago, IL: University of Chicago Press.

Burchell, R. W., , G. Lowenstein, W. R. Dolphin, C. Galley, A. Downs, S. Seskin, K. G. Still, T. Moore (2002). *The Costs of Sprawl—2000* (TRB Report No. 74). Washington, DC: National Academy Press.

Burchell, Robert W., N. A. Shad, D. Listokin, H. Phillips, A. Downs, S. Seskin, J. Davis, et al. (1998). *The Costs of Sprawl—Revisited* (TRB Report No. 39). Washington, DC: National Academy Press.

Calthorpe, P. (2010). *Urbanism in the Age of Climate Change.* Washington, DC: Island Press.

Carlino, G., S. Chatterjee, and R. Hunt (2006). Urban Density and the Rate of Invention. Federal Reserve Bank of Philadelphia. Working Paper 06-14, http://www .philadelphiafed.org/research-and-data/regional-economy/regional-research /index.cfm?tab=3.

Carruthers, J. I., and G. F. Ulfarsson (2003). Urban sprawl and the cost of public services. *Environment and Planning B: Planning and Design* 30: 503–522.

Cervero, R. (1998). *The Transit Metropolis: A Global Inquiry.* Washington, DC: Island Press.

Cervero, R., S. Murphy, C. Ferrell, N. Goguts, T.-H. Tsai, G. B. Arrington, J. Boroski, J. Smith-Heimer, R. Golem, P. Peninger, E. Nakajima, E. Chui, R. Dunphy, M. Myers, S. McKay, and N. Witenstein (2004). *Transit-Oriented Development in the United States: Experiences, Challenges, and Prospects.* TCRP Report 102. Washington, DC: National Academy Press.

Cervero, R. and S. Seskin (1995). *An Evaluation of the Relationships between Transit and Urban Form. Research Results Digest 7,* Transit Cooperative Research Program, Transportation Research Board, National Research Council.

Ciccone, A., and R. E. Hall (1996). Productivity and the density of economic activity. *American Economic Review,* 86(1): 54–70.

Cisneros, H., M. Dyer-Chamberlain, and J. Hickie (2012). *Independent for Life: Homes and Neighborhoods for an Aging America.* Austin, TX: University of Texas Press.

Chapple, K., J. Wegmann, A. Nemirow, and C. Dentel-Post (2012). *Yes in My Backyard: Mobilizing the Market for Secondary Units.* Berkeley, CA: Institute for Urban and Regional Development, University of California.

Christensen, J. (2008). *Big Box Reuse.* Cambridge, MA: MIT Press.

Cobb, R. J., and S. Dvorak (2000). Accessory Dwelling Units: Model State Act and Local Ordinance. Washington, DC: American Association of Retired Persons.

Condon, P. (2010). *Seven Rules for Sustainable Communities: Design Strategies for the Post-Carbon World.* Washington, DC: Island Press.

Congressional Budget Office (2009). *An Overview of Federal Support for Housing.* Washington, DC: US Congress.

Cortright, J. (2009). *Walking the Walk: How Walkability Raises Home Values in U.S Cities.* Washington, DC: CEOs for Cities. http://blog.walkscore.com/wp-content /uploads/2009/08/WalkingTheWalk_CEOsforCities.pdf.

Cowan, T. (2001). What is the Correct Intergenerational Discount Rate? Fairfax, VA: George Mason University, Department of Economics. http://www.gmu.edu /centers/publicchoice/faculty%20pages/Tyler/DISCOUNT.pdf.

Cudahy, Brian J. (1990). *Cash, Tokens, and Transfers: A History of Urban Mass Transit in North America.* New York: Fordham University Press.

Dalaker, Joseph (2001). *Poverty in the United States: 2000,* US Census Bureau, Current Population Reports, P60-214, US Government Printing Office, Washington, DC.

Dannenberg, A. L., H. Frumkin, and R. J. Jackson, eds. (2011). *Making Healthy Places: Designing and Building for Health, Well-being, and Sustainability.* Washington, DC: Island Press.

Day, J. C. (1996). *Projections of the Number of Households and Families in the United States: 1995 to 2010,* US Bureau of the Census, Current Population Reports, P25-1129, US Government Printing Office, Washington, DC.

DeNavas-Walt, C., B. D. Proctor, and J. C. Smith (2011). *Income, Poverty, and Health Insurance Coverage in the United States: 2010,* US Census Bureau, Current Population Reports, P60-239, US Government Printing Office, Washington, DC.

Dittmar, H., and G. Ohland (2003). *The New Transit Town: Best Practices in Transit-Oriented Development.* Washington, DC: Island Press.

Downs, A. (1973). *Open Up the Suburbs: A Strategy for Urban America.* New Haven, CT: Yale University Press.

Downs, B. (2003). *Fertility of American Women: June 2002.* US Census Bureau, Current Population Reports, P20-548. Washington, DC.

Dittmar, H., and G. Ohland, eds. (2003). *The New Transit Town: Best Practices in Transit-Oriented Development.* Island Press. Washington, DC.

Duany, A., E. Plater-Zyberk, and J. Speck. (2000). *Suburban Nation: The Rise of Sprawl and the Decline of the American Dream.* New York: North Point Press.

Dunham-Jones, E., and J. Williamson (2008). *Retrofitting Suburbia: Urban Design Solutions for Redesigning Suburbs.* New York: Wiley.

Dunphy, R., R. Cervero, F. Dock, M. McAvey, and D. R. Porter (2005). *Developing around Transit: Strategies and Solutions that Work.* Washington, DC: Urban Land Institute.

Eggers, F. J., and F. Moumen. (2011). *Housing Units that Serve Both the Renter and Owner Markets.* Washington, DC: US Department of Housing and Urban Development, Office of Policy Development and Research.

Energy Information Administration, US Department of Energy. (2006). Commercial Buildings Energy Consumption Survey 2003. http://www.eia.gov/emeu/cbecs/cbecs2003/detailed_tables_2003/detailed_tables_2003.html.

Energy Information Administration (2011). *EIA Weekly Petroleum Status Report.* (April 12) Washington, DC: US Department of Energy. Accessed April 24, 2011, http://www.eia.doe.gov/emeu/steo/pub/cf_query/steoNotes.cfm?formula=MGEIAUS&periodType=Annual&startYear=2000&startMonth=1&startQuarter=1&endYear=2012&endMonth=12&endQuarter=4.

Ewing, R. (2008). Highway-Induced Development: Results for Metropolitan Areas. *Transportation Research Record,* 2067: 101–109.

Ewing, R., R. Pendall, and D. Chen (2002). Measuring Sprawl and Its Impact. Washington, DC: Smart Growth America. http://www.smartgrowthamerica.org/resources/measuring-sprawl-and-its-impact/.

Ewing, R., T. Schmid, R. Killingsworth, A. Zlot, and S. Raudenbush (2003). Relationship between urban sprawl and physical activity, obesity, and morbidity. *American Journal of Health Promotion.* 18 (1): 47–57.

Ewing, R., K. Bartholomew, S. Winkelman, J. Walters, and D. Chen (2008). *Growing Cooler: Evidence on Urban Development and Climate Change*. Washington, DC: Urban Land Institute.

Faiola, A., E. Nakashima, and J. Drew (2008). What went wrong? *Washington Post*, October 15, http://www.washingtonpost.com/wp-dyn/content/article/2008/10/14/AR2008101403343.html?hpid=topnews&sid=ST2008101403344&s_pos=.

Farr, D. (2007). *Sustainable Urbanism: Urban Design With Nature*. New York: Wiley.

Federal Reserve Board (2012). *Changes in U.S. Family Finances from 2007 to 2010: Evidence from the Survey of Consumer Finances*, Washington, DC: Federal Reserve Board. http://www.federalreserve.gov/pubs/bulletin/2012/pdf/scf12.pdf.

Ferguson, R. F. and W. T. Dickens, eds. (1999), *Urban Problems and Community Development*. Washington, DC: Brookings Institution.

Frank, L., P. Engelke, and T. Schmid (2003). *Health and Community Design: The Impact of the Built Environment on Physical Activity*. Washington, DC: Island Press.

Freilich, R. H., and M. S. White (2008). *21st Century Land Development Code*. Chicago, IL: American Planning Association.

Frumkin, H., L. D. Frank, and R. Jackson (2004). *Urban Sprawl and Public Health: Designing, Planning, and Building for Healthy Communities*. Washington, DC: Island Press.

Glaeser, E. L. (2011). Goodbye, golden years. *New York Times*, November 19. http://www.nytimes.com/2011/11/20/opinion/sunday/retirement-goodbye-golden-years.html?pagewanted=all

Glaeser, E. L., and M. E. Kahn (2003). *Sprawl and Urban Growth*. Cambridge, MA: Harvard University, Harvard Institute of Economic Research. Discussion Paper Number 2004. http://www.economics.harvard.edu/pub/hier/2003/HIER2004.pdf.

Glaeser, E. L., and D. C. Mare (2001). Cities and skills. *Journal of Labor Economics* 19 (2): 316–342.

Golden, T. D., J. F. Veiga, and R. N. Dino. (2008). The impact of professional isolation on teleworker job performance and turnover intentions: Does time spent teleworking, interacting face-to-face, or having access to communication-enhancing technology matter? *Journal of Applied Psychology*, 93 (6): 1412–1421.

Goldin, C. (2004). The Long Road to the Fast Track: Career and Family, Mommies and Daddies on the Fast Track: Success of Parents in Demanding Professions, Special Issue of *Annals of the American Academy of Political and Social Science*, 596: 246–247.

Hamilton, B. E., J.A. Martin, S. J. Ventura (2009). Births: Preliminary data for 2007. *National Vital Statistics Reports*, Web release; 57 (12). Hyattsville, MD: National Center for Health Statistics. Released March 18, 2009.

Handy, S. L., M. G. Boarnet, R. Ewing, and R. E. Killingsworth (2002). How the built environment affects physical activity: Views from urban planning. *American Journal of Preventative Medicine* 23 (2 Suppl): 64–73.

Handy, S., J. Sallis, D. Weber, E. Maibach, and M. Hollander (2008). Is support for traditionally designed communities growing? Evidence from two national surveys. *Journal of the American Planning Association*, 74 (2): 209–221.

Harris, T. F., and Y. M. Ioannides (2002). *Productivity and Metropolitan Density*, Medford, MA: Tufts University, Department of Economics.

Harvard Joint Center for Housing Studies (2012). *The State of the Nation's Housing 2012.* Cambridge, MA: Harvard University.

Jackson, R. J. (2012). *Designing Healthy Communities.* New York: Jossey-Bass.

Jaffe, A. B., M. Trajtenberg, and R. Henderson (1993). Geographic localization of knowledge spillovers as evidenced by patent citations. *Quarterly Journal of Economics* 108 (3): 577–598.

Jonathan Rose Companies (2011). *Location Efficiency and Housing Type—Boiling it Down to BTUs.* Accessed March 25, 2011, http://epa.gov/smartgrowth/location _efficiency_BTU.htm.

Kamp, D. (2009). Rethinking the American Dream. *Vanity Fair.* http://www.vanity fair.com/culture/features/2009/04/american-dream200904.

Keenan, T. A. (2010). *Home and Community Preferences of the 45+ Population.* Washington, DC: American Association of Retired Persons.

Kneebone, E., and E. Garr (2010). *The Suburbanization of Poverty: Trends in Metropolitan America, 2000 to 2008.* Washington, DC: Brookings Institution.

Kreider, R. M., and R. Ellis (2011). *Number, Timing, and Duration of Marriages and Divorces: 2009* (Current Population Reports, P70-125). Washington, DC: US Census Bureau.

Kuzmyak, J. R., R. Weinberger, R. H. Pratt, and H. S. Levinson (2003). *Parking Management and Supply: Traveler Response to Transportation System Changes.* TCRP Report 95. Washington, DC: Transportation Research Board.

Lang, R. E. (2003). *Edgeless Cities.* Washington, DC: Brookings Institution.

Leinberger, C. B. (2007a). *Option of Urbanism.* Washington, DC: Island Press.

———. (2007b). *Back to the Future: The Need for Patient Equity in Real Estate Development Finance.* Washington, DC: Brookings Institution.

———. (2008). The Next Slum? The subprime crisis is just the tip of the iceberg. *The Atlantic.* Accessed July 24, 2012, http://www.theatlantic.com/magazine/archive /2008/03/the-next-slum/6653/.

———. (2010). Here Comes the Neighborhood, *Atlantic*, June, accessed February 19, 2011, http://www.theatlantic.com/magazine/archive/2010/06/here -comes-the-neighborhood/8093/

Lennertz, B., and A. Lutzenhiser (2006). *The Charrette Handbook.* Chicago: American Planning Association.

Levine, J. (2005). *Zoned Out: Regulation, Markets, and Choices in Transportation and Metropolitan Land Use.* Baltimore, MD: Resources for the Future.

Li, F., P. Harmer, B. J. Cardinal, M. Bosworth, D. Johnson-Shelton, J. M. Moore, A. Acock, and N. Vongjaturapat (2009). Built environment and 1-year change in weight and waist circumference in middle-aged and older adults: Portland Neighborhood Environment and Health Study. *American Journal of Epidemiology* 169 (4): 409–412; discussion 413–414. http://www.ncbi.nlm.nih.gov/pubmed /19153213?itool=EntrezSystem2.PEntrez.Pubmed.Pubmed_ResultsPanel .Pubmed_RVAbstract.

Litman, T. (2006). *Smart Growth Policy Reforms.* Victoria, BC: Victoria Transportation Policy Institute. Accessed July 24, 2012, http://www.vtpi.org/smart_growth _reforms.pdf.

———. (2009). *Evaluating Transportation Economic Development Impacts: Understanding How Transportation Policies and Planning Decisions Affect Productivity, Employ-*

*ment, Business Activity, Property Values and Tax Revenues*, Victoria, BC: Victoria Transport Policy Institute, http://www.vtpi.org/econ_dev.pdf.

———. (2010). *Land Use Impacts on Transportation*. Victoria, BC: Victoria Transport Policy Institute, http://www.vtpi.org/landtravel.pdf.

———. (2012). *Evaluating Criticism of Smart Growth*. Victoria, BC: Victoria Transport Policy Institute. http://www.vtpi.org/sgcritics.pdf.

Lodl, K. A., B. S. Gabb, and E. Raedene Combs (2005). The importance of selected housing features at various stages of the life cycle. *Journal of Family and Economic Issues* 11 (4): 383–395. http://www.springerlink.com/content/nw17q263j177 mg46/.

Lucas, R. E., Jr., and E. Rossi-Hansberg (2002). On the internal structure of cities. *Econometrica* 70 (4): 1445–1476.

Malloy, R. P. (2008). Private Property, Community Development, and Eminent Domain. Aldershott, UK: Ashgate.

Marks, S. G. (2011). *Valuing the Future: Intergenerational Discounting, its Problems, and a Modest Proposal*. Boston Univ. School of Law Working Paper No. 11-12. http://ssrn.com/abstract=1783729.

Martin, J. A., B. E. Hamilton, P. D. Sutton, and S. J. Ventura (2009). *Final Data for 2006: National Vital Statistics Reports*, 57 (7) Hyattsville, MD: National Center for Health Statistics.

Mathur, S., and C. E. Ferrell (2009). *Effect of Suburban Transit-Oriented Developments on Residential Property Values*. San José, CA: Mineta Transportation Institute, San José State University. http://www.transweb.sjsu.edu/MTIportal/research /publications/documents/Effects%20of%20Sub-Urban%20Transit%20%28 with%20Cover%29.pdf.

McCann, B. A. and R. Ewing (2003). *Measuring the Health Effects of Sprawl*. Washington, DC: Smart Growth America. http://www.smartgrowthamerica.org/report /HealthSprawl8.03.pdf.

McIlwain, J. (2009). *Housing in America: The Next Decade*. Washington, DC: Urban Land Institute.

McKeever, M. (2011). *White Paper on Changing National Demographics and Demand for Housing Types*. Sacramento, CA: Sacramento Area Council of Governments.

Mertens, J.-F. and A. Rubinchick (2006). *Intergenerational Equity and the Discount Rate for Cost-Benefit Analysis*. Philadelphia, PA: University of Pennsylvania, Department of Economics. http://economics.sas.upenn.edu/events/intergenerational -equity-and-discount-rate-cost-benefit-analsis.

Minadeo, D. F. (2009). *Price Premiums and Mixed-Use Development*. Washington, DC: NAIOP Research Foundation. http://www.naiop.org/foundation/CTMTMixedUse Research.pdf.

Mokhtarian, P. L., I. Salomon, and S. Choo. (2005). Measuring the unmeasurable: Why can't we agree on the number of telecommuters in the US? *Quality & Quantity*, 39 (4): 423–452. Univ. California, Davis, http://escholarship.org/uc/item /7mb104c1.

Molloy, R., and H. Shan (2011). *The Effect of Gasoline Prices on Household Location*. Washington, DC: Federal Reserve Board. https://federalreserve.gov/pubs/feds /2010/201036/201036pap.pdf.

Myers, D., and E. Gearin (2001). Current preferences and future demand for denser residential environments. *Housing Policy Debate* 12 (4): 633–659.

Myers, D., and S. H. Ryu. (2008). Aging of the baby boomers and the generational housing bubble: Foresight and mitigation of an epic transition. *Journal of the American Planning Association* 74 (1): 17–33.

National Alliance of Public Transportation Advocates. 2008. *Mobility for the Aging Population*. Washington, DC.

National Center for Educational Statistics (2009). *Achievement Gaps How Black and White Students in Public Schools Perform in Mathematics and Reading on the National Assessment of Educational Progress*. Washington, DC: US Department of Education.

———. (2011). *Achievement Gaps: How Hispanic and White Students in Public Schools Perform in Mathematics and Reading on the National Assessment of Educational Progress*. Washington, DC: US Department of Education.

Nelson, A.C. (1992). Effects of heavy-rail transit stations on house prices with respect to neighborhood income. *Transportation Research Record*, 1359: 127–132.

———. (1995). *System Development Charges for Water, Wastewater, and Stormwater Systems*, Los Angeles: Los Angeles Times Publishing.

———. (1999). Transit stations and commercial property values. *Journal of Public Transportation*, 2 (3): 77–96.

———. (2001). Exclusionary housing, urban sprawl, and smart growth. *Georgia State University Law Review*. 17(4): 1087–1102.

———. (2004). *Planners' Estimating Guide: Estimating Land-Use and Facility Needs*. Chicago: American Planning Association.

———. (2006). Leadership in a new era. *Journal of the American Planning Association* 72 (4): 393–407.

———. (2009a). The new urbanity: The rise of a new America. *Annals of the Academy of Political and Social Science* 626: 192–208.

———. (2009b). Demographic outlook for multi-family housing. *Multifamily Trends*. Nov/Dec.

———. (2010). Catching the next wave. *Generations: Journal of Aging and Society*. 33 (4).

Nelson, A. C., and C. J. Dawkins (2004). *Urban Containment in the United States*. Chicago: American Planning Association.

Nelson, A. C., and S. J. McClesky (1990). Elevated rapid rail station impacts on single-family house values. *Transportation Research Record* 1266: 173–180.

Nelson, A. C., and M. Moody (2000). Effect of beltways on metropolitan economic activity. *Journal of Urban Planning and Development* 126 (4): 189–196.

Nelson, A. C., T. W. Sanchez, and C. J. Dawkins. (2004). Urban containment and residential segregation: a preliminary investigation. *Urban Studies* 41(2): 423–440.

Nelson, A. C., C. J. Dawkins, and T. W. Sanchez. (2005). The effect of urban containment and mandatory housing elements on racial segregation in US metropolitan areas. *Journal of Urban Affairs* 26 (3): 339–350.

Nelson, A. C., Dawkins, C. J., and T. W. Sanchez (2007). *Urban Containment and Society*. Hampshire, UK: Ashgate.

Nelson, A. C., G. Anderson, K. Bartholomew, P. Perlich, T. W. Sanchez, and R. Ewing (2009). *The Best Stimulus for the Money*. Washington, DC: Smart Growth America.

Norman, J., H. L. MacLean, and C. A. Kennedy (2006). Comparing high and low residential density: Life-cycle analysis of energy use and greenhouse gas emissions. *Journal of Urban Planning and Development* 132 (1): 10–21.

Norris, N. (2012). Why Gen Y is causing the Great Migration of the 21st century. *Better! Cities & Towns,* April 12, http://bettercities.net/news-opinion/blogs/nathan-norris/17803/why-gen-y-causing-great-migration-21st-century.

Parolek, D. G., K. Parolek, and P. C. Crawford (2008). *Form-Based Codes: A Guide for Planners, Urban Designers, Municipalities, and Developers*. New York: Wiley.

Parsons Brinckerhoff Quade and Douglas, Inc. (1996). *Transit and Urban Form*. TCRP Report 16, Vol. 2. Washington, DC: National Academy Press.

Peiser, R. (2007). *Regenerating Older Suburbs*. Washington, DC: The Urban Land Institute.

Perk, V. A., and M. Catalá (2009). *Land Use Impacts of Bus Rapid Transit: Effects of BRT Station Proximity on Property Values along the Pittsburgh Martin Luther King, Jr. East Busway*. Tampa, FL: National Bus Rapid Transit Institute, Center for Urban Transportation Research, University of South Florida. http://www.nbrti.org/docs/pdf/Property%20Value%20Impacts%20of%20BRT_NBRTI.pdf.

Pew Research Center (2010). The Return of the Multi-Generational Family Household. Washington, DC: Pew Charitable Trusts. Accessed July 24, 2012, http://www.pewsocialtrends.org/2010/03/18/the-return-of-the-multi-generational-family-household/.

Phillips, J., R. Beasley, and A. Rodgers (2005). District of Columbia Population and Housing Trends. Washington, DC: City of Washington, DC. Accessed July 24, 2012, http://www.neighborhoodinfodc.org/pdfs/demographic_trends05.pdf.

Pitkin, J., and D. Myers (2008). *U.S. Housing Trends—Generational Changes and the Outlook to 2050*. Transportation Research Board Special Report 298. Washington, DC: National Academy of Sciences.

Pollakowski, H. O., D. Ritchay, and Z. Weinrobe. (2005). *Effects of Mixed-Income, Multi-Family Rental Housing Developments on Single Family Housing Values*. Cambridge, MA: MIT Center for Real Estate. http://web.mit.edu/cre/research/hai/pdf/40B_report_HAI_0405.pdf.

Porter Novelli Public Services (2003, 2005). *ConsumerStyles*. Washington, DC.

Portland, City of (2008). *Portland Streetcar Development Oriented Transit,* http://www.portlandstreetcar.org/pdf/development_200804_report.pdf.

Rabianski, J. S., and J. S. Clements (2007). *Mixed-Use Development: A Review of Professional Literature*. Washington, DC: National Association of Office and Industrial Parks. http://www.naiop.org/foundation/rabianski.pdf.

Randolph, J. R. (2008). *Energy for Sustainability: Technology, Planning, Policy*. Washington, DC: Island Press.

RCLCO (2008). Measuring the Market for Green Residential Development. Bethesda, MD: RCLCO. Accessed July 23, 2012, http://www.rclco.com/pdf/Measuring_the_Market.pdf.

———. (2011). *Smart Growth Survey Analysis*. Bethesda, MD: RCLCO.

Rohe, W. M. and H. L. Watson, eds. (2007). *Chasing the American Dream: New Perspectives on Affordable Homeownership*. Ithaca, NY: Cornell University Press.

Russell, J. S. (2011). *The Agile City: Building Well-being and Wealth in an Era of Climate Change*. Washington, DC: Island Press.

Sanchez, T. W. (1999). The connection between public transit and employment: The cases of Portland and Atlanta. *Journal of the American Planning Association* 65 (3): 284–296.

Schmitz, A. (2003). *The New Shape of Suburbia*. Washington, DC: Urban Land Institute.

Schwartz, A. (2007). *Housing Policy in the United States*. New York: Routledge.

Slone, D.K., D. S. Goldstein, and W. A. Gowder (2008). *A Legal Guide to Urban and Sustainable Development for Planners, Developers, and Architects*. New York: Wiley.

Steiner, C. (2009). *$20 Per Gallon: How the Inevitable Rise in the Price of Gasoline Will Change Our Lives for the Better*. New York: Grand Central.

Surface Transportation Planning Process (2005). *Driven to Spend: Pumping Dollars out of Our Households and Communities*, Center for Neighborhood Technology. http://www.transact.org/library/reports_pdfs/driven_to_spend/Driven_to _Spend_Report.pdf.

Sutton, P. C., and R. Costanza (2002). Global estimates of market and non-market values derived from nighttime satellite imagery, land cover, and ecosystem service valuation. *Ecological Economics* 41: 509–527.

Thomas, J. (2010). *Residential Construction Trends in America's Metropolitan Regions*. Washington, DC: Environmental Protection Agency.

Tombari, E. A. (2005). Mixed-Use Development. Washington, DC: National Association of Home Builders.

Transportation for America (2011). *Aging in Place, Stuck without Options: Fixing the Mobility Crisis Threatening the Baby Boom Generation*. Washington, DC: Transportation for America.

Trulia-Harris Interactive Survey (2010). *Infographics for Trulia's August 2010 American Dream Survey*. Accessed July 24, 2012, info.trulia.com/index.php?s=32055 &item=106116.

Tu, C. C., and M. J. Eppli (1999). *Valuing New Urbanism: The Case of Kentlands. Real Estate Economics* 23 (3): 425–451.

Tuttle, B. (2012). Getting real: E-tailers discover the virtues of brick-and-mortar stores. *Time Magazine*. March 12. p. 23. http://www.time.com/time/magazine /article/0,9171,2108039,00.html.

United Nations (2009). *Planning Sustainable Cities—Global Report on Human Settlements 2009*. New York: United Nations. Accessed July 23, 2012, http://www .unhabitat.org/content.asp?typeid=19&catid=555&cid=5607.

Urban Land Institute (2010a). *Place Making through Infill and Corridor Redevelopment*. Washington, DC: Urban Land Institute.

———. (2010b). *SB 375 Impact Analysis Report*. Washington, DC: Urban Land Institute.

———. (2011). *What's Next? Real Estate in the New Economy*. Washington, DC: Urban Land Institute.

US Department of Housing and Urban Development (HUD) (2010). *American Housing Survey for 2009*. Washington, DC: US Government Printing Office.

———. (2011). American Housing Survey for the United States: 2009. Washington, DC: US Government Printing Office.

US Environmental Protection Agency (2007). *Measuring the Air Quality and Transportation Impacts of Infill Development*. Washington, DC. http://www.epa.gov/dced/pdf/transp_impacts_infill.pdf.

Voith, R. (1998). Parking, transit, and employment in a central business district. *Journal of Urban Economics* 44 (1): 43–48.

Wapshott, R., and O. Mallett (2012). The spatial implications of homeworking. *Organization* 19: 63.

Wheeler, C. H. (2005). *Cities and the Growth of Wages among Young Workers*. St. Louis, MO: Federal Research Board of St. Louis. Working Paper 2005-055A. http://research.stlouisfed.org/wp/2005/2005-055.pdf.

Williamson, J. (forthcoming). Designing Suburban Futures. Washington, DC: Island Press.

Wilson, A., and R. Navaro (2007). Driving to green buildings: The transportation energy intensity of buildings. *Environmental Building News*, 16 (9) http://www.buildinggreen.com/auth/article.cfm?fileName=160901a.xml.

Woods & Poole Economics (2010, 2011), *The Complete Economic and Demographic Data Source*, Washington, DC.

Zhu, X. D., N. McArdle, and G. S. Masnick (2001). *Second Homes: What, How Many, Where and Who*. Cambridge, MA: Joint Center for Housing Studies, Harvard University.

# INDEX

Boxes, figures, and tables are indicated by page number followed by b, f, or t respectively.

Accessory dwelling units (ADU), 65, 117, 127n17
Adjustable rate mortgages (ARMs), 12
Affordable housing, 65, 104–6
Agglomeration economies, 96–99, 100
Aging in place, 22, 38
Aging trends, 17
Altoon, R. A., 115
American Dream, home ownership and, 1, 9, 15
American Housing Survey, 3, 28, 44
Atlanta, Georgia, 4, 119, 126n14
Attached housing, 2–3, 42, 95, 118–19
Auld, J. C., 115
Automobile congestion, 30, 100

Baby Boom Century, 35
Baby Boom generation
  aging trends and, 17
  in demographic changes, 21
  end of America's youth movement, 51
  generational characteristics, 22
  housing market influence, 33
  housing market shifts, 36
  in key trends facing real estate industry, 31
  multigenerational households and, 27
  over-sixty-five population, 5
  population increase and, 124n18

retirement age, 18–19
single-family homes on large lots and, 109
single-person households and, 27
Bartholomew, K., 101-2, 112
Beltways, and losses in retail and service sales, 98
Building energy use, 94–95
Burchell, R., 104

Calthorpe, P., 113
Car-based transportation, low-income families and, 106–7
Carbon emissions, 95–96
Car independence, 45
Car-oriented residential development, and city density, 2
Central cities, residential construction in, 4, 122
Cervero, R., 115
Charter schools, 46
Children, dependency ratios for, 20t
Christensen, J., 114
Commercial property values, transit system proximity and, 102
Commercial uses, energy consumption, 94
Communities
  creating healthier, 113
  live-work-play, 45

143

Communities (*cont.*)
master-planned, 109–10
new urbanism, 91
smart growth, 3
sustainable, 112–16
walkable, 3
Compact development benefits, 106–8,
110
Condominiums, 118
Condon, P., 112
Construction permits, discipline in
issuance of, 121
Conventional lots, 2–3, 42, 63–65
CoreNet Global, 73

Dannenberg, A. L., 113
Dawkins, C. J., 105, 107
Demographic trends, 21–27
Density
economic agglomeration and, 98–99
employment and, 95–97
Gen Y and, 45
lower, car-oriented residential
development and, 2
mortality rates and, 107–8
public transit and, 42
vehicle miles traveled (VMT) and, 95
Dependency ratios, 17–21, 20t
Dittmar, H., 115
Downsized housing, 31, 33, 53, 56
Dunham-Jones, E., 114
Dunphy, R. R., 115

E-commerce, 69–70, 74–75, 128n13
Economic agglomeration, 96–99, 100
Economic benefits of reshaping
America, 3–4, 96–104
Economic resilience, population density
and, 97
Economic value of open spaces, 92–93
Education, and housing, 35, 46, 61–63
Eisenhower generation, 21
Emerging market-based demand,
benefits of meeting, 3–4
Employment
density, 95–97
projections, 67–69

public transit and, 99
space-occupying, 67–71, 70t
teleworking pros and cons, 72–73
trends, 11, 69
Energy consumption, 93–95
Energy costs, 9–10, 30, 46
Environmental benefits of reshaping
America, 3–4, 92–96
Ewing, R., 95, 99, 101-2, 107–8
Exclusionary zoning, local, 119

Family net worth, demographic changes
in, 10
Farr, D., 113
Fatalities in highest vs. lowest
residential density areas, 108
Federal tax code, 117–18
Federal underwriting, in housing
finance, 118
Fertility rates, increase in, 26
Fiscal bases, local
weakening of, as key trend facing real
estate industry, 31–32
Floor-area ratio (FAR), defined, 30
Foreclosures, 65, 103
Fossil fuel consumption, 94
Frank, L. P., 113
Freilich, R. H., 116
Frumkin, H., 113
Future county migration, 124n16

Gaithersburg, Maryland, 129n1
Gasoline prices, major market trends, 10
Gen X, 22, 52
Gen Y
dependency trends and, 17
and future household composition,
52
generational characteristics, 22
housing, transportation, and lifestyle
preferences, 42–45
housing market influence, 33–34
importance of walkability and
bikability to, 39
in key trends facing real estate
industry, 31
as next big market, 44–46

Great Depression, and housing values, 4

Great Recession
  development patterns in aftermath of, 1
  and home equity decline, 12
  household size and, 48
  lending institutions and, 12–13
  and loss of real estate equity, 101–2
  multigenerational households and, 51
  overbuilding of residential stock and, 6
  and shifting wealth, 11–12
  and trend toward working at home, 71–72

Great Senior Sell-Off, 35–36

Health care, projected job growth, 69
Herbert, Chris, 111
Highway investments, 100
Hispanics, and population growth, 25–26
Home buyers, changing profile of, 63–65
Home construction (2000s), 51

Home ownership
  down-payment requirements for, 13
  major market trends, 9–11
  shift in attitudes toward, 13–14
  subsidies for, 117–18
  waning institutional support for, 12–15

Home ownership rates
  among selected racial/ethnic groups (2000-2010), 58f
  changes in (1940-2010), 2
  compared (1950-2010), 61
  decline in 2000s, 61
  education gap and differences in, 61–63
  estimated (2030), 63
  highest (2004-2005), 51
  projected (2020), 14–15
  reasons for decline in, 61

Home values
  expectations based on growth rates and location, 29t

  factors in resilience of, during economic downturns, 102
  market trends, 13

Household composition
  by age group, 52–57
  with children, 52, 53t
  in demographic changes, 21
  Millenials and, 52
  by race/ethnicity, 57–59
  racial, 24
  by type, 51–52, 53t
  without children, 21, 24, 27, 52, 53t

Household income
  demographic changes and, 10–11
  education and, 61–62
  in key trends facing real estate industry, 30
  low, and car-based transportation, 106–7
  median (1975-2010), 54f
  median (1993-2007), 53
  mortgage underwriting and, 119
  walking and biking accessibility preference and, 39

Households and householders
  declining propensity to relocate by people age 35 to 54, 125n7
  defined, 47
  life cycle of, 53–54
  share of change in, by age category (1990-2010), 56t
  share of change in, by age category (2010-2030), 57t
  share of change in 35-64 age category compared to all (1970-1975 and 2005-2010), 55f

Household size
  Baby Boomers and, 53
  changes in, 48–51
  comparison (2000, 2010), 51
  by decade (1900-2010), 48t
  declining (1900-2000), 25
  declining, and suburbanization, 49
  declining, in Washington, D.C., 49
  reasons for increases in, 26
  stabilization of, 49–50

Household size (*cont.*)
trend change in, 25–26
trends and projections, 51
Housing
affordable, 65
affordable housing vs. creating equity
in, 104–6
changes in stock of (1985-2009), 28
construction needs, for nation and
census regions and divisions, 62t
distribution of choice options (2006),
42
education and, 61–62
excess (2010), 126n9
location costs, 119
lost and replaced, 60–61
as percent of household costs, 103
preferences of Baby Boomers and
Gen Y, 1
preferred size (2011), 2
relationship betwen commute time
and size of, 35
Housing crisis, impact of, 13–14
Housing demand
Baby Boomers and new, 36
emerging market-based, benefits of
meeting, 3–4
family-based, 58
generational projections, 23–24
infill and redevelopment in meeting
new, 82–83
by location and rent vs. purchase
(2010-2030), 27–28
by major household age group,
54–56
in new market, 27–29, 109
preference by type, 42–44
and supply, 41–44, 44t, 61
triple storm of motive-means-
opportunity, 53–54
type and quantity for 2030, 81
Housing finance, 91, 118
Housing supply, mismatch with
demand, 41–44, 44t
Housing tenure, 61–63
Housing tenure demand (2010-2030),
64t

Housing units
change in features (1989-2009), 55t
total needed (2030), 59–60

iGeneration, 23, 124n18
Income levels
agglomeration economies and, 98
Individual retirement accounts, 19–21
Industrial job growth, 69
Industrial uses
energy consumption and, 94
Infill development
fiscal benefits, 103–4
and lower carbon emissions, 95–96
in meeting demand for new
development, 82
in reshaping metropolitan America,
93
Innovation
population density and, 97
Institution job growth, 69
Integrated land uses
in new urbanism, 37
Intergenerational value, 93
Internet retailing, 69–70
Internet substitution of retail space,
74–75

Jackson, R. J., 113
Job, defined, 69
Jobs, allocation into land-use categories,
68b
Jobs-housing balance, in compact vs.
sprawling areas, 107
Joint Center for Housing Studies,
Harvard University, 111

Kentlands, Gaithersburg, Maryland,
129n1

Land appreciation rate, compared to
depreciation rate of nonresidential
structures, 75–77
Land use, urban and urban-related
(1987-2007), 92–93
Land use and development patterns
(1950-1990), 2

Land use intensity, assumptions in RAI, 84

Land use policies
affordable housing and, 105
local, and inefficient redevelopment, 86
reforming, 115–16

Lang, R. E., 86

Large-lot options, 2–3, 63–65

Leinberger, C. B., 37, 65, 127n14

Litman, T., 89, 90, 95-6, 106,

Life cycle of households, 53–54

Lifespan of major building classes before cycling, 77f

Live-work-play communities, 45

Living space in single-family detached homes (1989, 2009), 54

Lodging industry job growth, 69

London Interbank Offered Rate (LIBOR), 12

Lot size
average, for detached single-family homes, 97
conventional, 2–3, 42, 63–65
and living space, single-family detached homes, 54
in master-planned communities, 109–10
small, 2–3, 42

Low-income families, car-based transportation, 106–7

Low-rise nonresidential structures, 82–83

Market preferences
of Baby Boomers, 1, 36
Gen Y and, 1, 42–45
for housing by type, 42–44
for public transit, 3, 37, 41, 91–92
for smart growth attributes, 34, 39
stated vs. revealed, 91–92
for walkability and bikability, 3, 34–35

Market trends, accommodation of, 5, 116

McCann, B.A., 107–8

McIlwain, J., 14, 51

McMansions, 65

Millenials, 17, 22–23, 52

Minorities, racial and ethnic
in 2040s, 57–58
in demographic changes, 21
education gap and differences in home ownership rates, 61–63
Hispanics and population growth, 25–26
percent change in population and household size (2010-2030), 59
population of, 19t, 25–26, 59
population of, in the nation, census regions and divisions (2010-2030), 19t
trends, 17

Mixed-income and mixed-housing neighborhoods
revealed preference for, 91

Mixed-use and mixed-housing developments
property values and, 102

Mixed-use developments, revealed preference for, 92

Mobility options, in compact vs. sprawling areas, 106–7

Mortality rates, in higher density cities vs. sprawling urban areas, 107

Mortgages
adjustable rate (ARMs), 12
education and incomes adequate to afford, 61–62
financial market for underwriting, 13
subprime, 12
underwriting, 119

Multifamily development demand, 31

Multigenerational households
demographic and cultural shifts and growth in, 50–51
growth in, and stabilization of household size, 49–50
and increasing household size, 26–27
percent population living in (1900-2008), 50f
projected increase in, 28
trends and projections, 51

Multimodal options, and agglomeration economies, 100

Nashville, Tennessee, 114
National Association of Home Builders, 13
National Association of Realtors (NAR) survey, 2, 34, 43–44
National Center for Educational Statistics, 63
National Foundation for Credit Counseling survey, 13–14
National Household Travel Survey, 39–40
Neighborhood and community attributes
Baby Boomer preferences, 36
in new urbanism, 38
Neighborhood preservation, 84–86
Nelson, A. C. xi, 2, 6, 33, 36-8, 42–4, 59–60, 73-4, 98, 102, 105, 107, 119
New urbanism communities, 35–38, 91
NIMBY (not in my backyard), 83, 114, 116
Nonresidential, nonindustrial space, 71
Nonresidential land uses, net change to inventory, 79t
Nonresidential space
durability of, 75
factors in speed of recycling, 75–77
new, replaced, and repurposed, 1
in reshaping America, 4–5, 80
ripeness for renewal (2010-2030), 30
as share of built environment, 67
supported, net additions to inventory, and replaced/repurposed space, 79t
transit corridors and nodes, 110
trends that could result in reductions in, 71–80
Nonresidential structures
average life of, 77
depreciation rate of, compared to appreciation rate of land, 75–77
low-rise, 82–83
population growth rate and pace of replacement/repurposing of, 78–79

redevelopment ripeness by 2030, 81–82
ripeness for recycling, 77–79
North American Industry Classification System (NAICS), 67, 68b

Office group job growth, 69
Office hotelling, 69–71
Office spaces, shrinking, 73–74
Ohland, G., 115
Open spaces, 92–93, 129n4
Ozone levels, 108

Parking lot redevelopment, 82–83, 113–15
Parking requirements, in local land use policies, 86
Parolek, D. G., 116
Peak-demand households, share of change in (1990-2010), 56–57
Peiser, R., 114
Planners, challenges facing, 65
Planning and community design, new paradigm of, 112
Planning Sustainable Cities (United Nations), 112
Policies to reshape America, 116–21
Population
age distribution, 24
Baby Boom generation and increase in, 124n18
density of, and economic resilience, 97
by generation (2010-2030), 23t
Gen Y and preference for density, 45
growth rate and pace of nonresidential structure replacement/repurposing, 78–79
job growth compared to growth in, 69
of the nation, census regions and divisions (2010-2030), 16t
projections, 124n16
seniors (2010-2030), 18t
trends (2010-2030), 16–21, 16t
Porter-Novelli, 39, 125n6

Portland, Oregon, 101
Poverty rate, demographic changes, 10
Preferences, stated vs. revealed, 91–92
Production speed, population density and, 97
Property taxes, 118
Property values, 101–3, 115
Public facilities, financing subsidies and pricing schemes, 119–20
Public health, 107–8
Public policies, 65, 91, 111, 116–17, 119–20
Public transit
    access to, and labor participation rates, 106
    compact land use and, 110
    in corridor-based redevelopment, 115
    corridors and nodes, and new residential and nonresidential development, 110
    economic benefits of investments in, 101
    employment and, 99
    enhanced agglomeration economies and, 100
    in key trends facing real estate industry, 31
    minimum detached residential unit density to support, 42
    preference for proximity to, 41
    preferences for options (2008), 3
    property values and proximity to, 102–3
    revealed preference for, 91
    revealed preference for station proximity, 92
    seniors' preference for access to, 37

Racial and ethnic minorities. See Minorities, racial and ethnic
Racial integration, in compact vs. sprawling areas, 107
Rail transit and bus rapid transit proximity
    revealed preference for, 91

RCLCO (Robert Charles Lesser and Co.), 34, 42–44
Real estate equity, 101–2
Real estate industry
    key trends (2010-2030), 30–32
Recycling ripeness of fifty-year depreciation structures, 78f
Redevelopment
    fiscal benefits, 103–4
    and lower carbon emissions, 95–96
    in meeting demand for new development, 82–83
    property values and, 115
    in reshaping metropolitan America, 93
    timely, roadblocks to, 86
Regional approach to redevelopment, 110–11
Relocation, propensity for, by age group, 125n7
Rental housing, projected demand, 15
Renter-based subsidies, 118
Renting vs. owning, Gen Y and, 45
Repurposing older structures, 84–86
Reshape America Index (RAI), 83–84, 85t
Reshaping America
    business-as-usual vs., 90t
    decision-making processes, 116
    economic benefits of, 3–4, 96–104
    environmental benefits of, 3–4, 92–96
    guidance for, 110–11
    nonresidential space in, 4–5, 80
    policies for, 116–21
    social benefits of, 104–8
Residential development, new, 4, 110, 122
Residential property values, transit system proximity and, 102
Residential units, new and replaced, 1, 83–84
Residential uses, energy consumption and, 94
Retail and service sales, in agglomeration economies, 98

Retail e-commerce, 74–75
Retail job growth, 69
Robert Charles Lesser and Co (RCLCO).
    See RCLCO (Robert Charles Lesser
    and Co.)
Russell, J. S., 112–13

Sanchez, T. W., 106
Savings and loan industry, commercial
    space overbuilding and, 6
Schmitz, A., 114
Self-employed people, 71
Senior housing, types, 125n2
Seniors
    aging trends and, 17
    in dependency ratios, 20t
    dependency ratios for the nation,
        census regions and divisions, 20t
    population for the nation, census
        regions and divisions (2010-2030),
        18t
    reasons for not relocating, 38
    retirement age, 18–19
    sale of homes by, 36–37
Short sales, 127n15
Single-family homes, detached
    average lot size (2009), 97
    Baby Boom generation and demand
        for, 109
    energy consumption by, compared to
        energy-efficient attached home, 94
    square feet of living space and lot size
        (1989, 2009), 54
Single-person households, 24, 27, 52,
    53t
Small lots, 2–3, 42
Smart growth attributes
    market preferences for, 34, 39
Smart growth communities, 3
Smart growth vs. sprawl
    in NAR survey, 34
Smart growth websites, 121
Social benefits
    of meeting emerging market
        demands, 3–4
Social benefits of reshaping America,
    104–8

Social engineering, 117–19
Social services
    job growth projected in, 69
South Atlantic census division, 84
Space needs per worker
    assumptions (2010-2030), 74
    estimating, 75
Space occupied per office worker
    technology and reductions in, 73
Space-occupying employment
    for the nation and census regions and
        divisions (2010-2030), 70t
    projections, 67–71
Space-occupying jobs, 67
Spaces with redevelopment potential
attributes of, 82–83
Sprawl
    and adverse public health outcomes,
        107
    and chronic disease, 108
    and reduced productivity, 98
Sprawl costs, 104
Sprawl index, 107
Square feet of space consumed per
        industrial worker and
        nonindustrial worker
        estimated, 76t
Starter-home households
    share of change in (1990-2010), 56
State of the Nation's Housing, The (Joint
    Center for Housing Studies), 111
Stone, D. K., 115–16
Subprime mortgages, 12, 126n4
Suburbanization, 1–2, 35, 49
Suburbs
    blight and redevelopment, in key
        trends facing real estate industry,
        31
    demographic changes in, 11
    redevelopment and retrofitting,
        86–87
    in reshaping America, 93
    revitalizing, 110–11
Surveys
    American Housing Survey, 3, 28, 44
    National Association of Realtors, 2,
        34, 43–44

National Foundation for Credit Counseling, 13–14
National Household Travel Survey, 39–40
Sustainable communities, guiding principles, 112–16

Teleworking/telecommuting and working at home, 70–73
Transit-oriented developments (TODs), 101, 115
See also Public transit
Transportation
and cost of location, 119
elevating economic returns from investment in, 99–101
energy consumption and, 94
equity in, 106–7
in housing expenses, 119
investments in, to increase settlement density, 96–97
as percent of household costs, 103

Unemployment, public transit and, 99
Urban containment policies, affordable rental housing and, 105–6
Urban Land Institute (ULI), 28, 30–32, 110–11
Urban redevelopment, shift to the suburbs, 110–11
US Bureau of Economic Analysis, 69

Value of real property, as source of wealth, 101–2

Vehicle miles traveled (VMT), 93, 95–96

Walkability and bikability, 39–41
compact land use and, 110
defined, 125n5
importance of, 40, 40t
in key trends facing real estate industry, 31, 32
in new urbanism, 37
preference for, 3, 34–35
preference for, revealed, 91
walking or biking trips (1995-2009), 41t
Walk Score, 129n2
Washington, D.C., 49
Wealth, 11–12, 101–2
See also Household income
White, M. S., 116
Whites, in demographic changes, 21
Williamson, J., 114
Woods & Poole Economics, Inc., 16–21, 48, 67–69, 124n16
Working at home and teleworking/telecommuting, 70–73
World War II, end of, and home ownership, 9

YIMBY (yes in my backyard), 83, 114

Zoning codes, 111, 117, 119